Complete
Starter Guide to
Macramé

ISBN 978-1-4971-0494-5

Library of Congress Control Number: 2024948477

To learn more about the other great books from Fox Chapel Publishing, or to find a retailer near you, call toll-free at 800-457-9112, send mail to 903 Square Street, Mount Joy, PA 17552, or visit us at www.FoxChapelPublishing.com.

We are always looking for talented authors. To submit an idea, please send a brief inquiry to acquisitions@foxchapelpublishing.com.

Printed in the United States of America

Complete
Starter Guide to
Macramé

15 Knotted Home Creations Made with Natural Materials

Angela Barretta

FOX CHAPEL
PUBLISHING

Contents

Introduction   6

Gallery   8

Getting Started   22

Supplies and Tools   22

Knot and Pattern Guide   26

Tips and Tricks   44

Wall Hangings   47

Celeste Wall Hanging   48

Tree of Life Wall Hanging   54

Shiloh Feather Wall Hanging   60

Mushroom Wall Hanging   66

Leo Mountain Dyed Wall Hanging   72

Haven Wall Cat Bed   78

Plant Hangers   85

Ayla Plant Hanger   86

Merek Plant Hanger   90

Ariah Plant Hanger   94

Coralynn Wall Plant Hanger   98

Fruit Hangers   103

Fruit Hammock   104

Hanging Fruit Basket   107

Beaded Banana Hanger   112

Shelves   115

Arvin Wall Shelf   116

Stella Jewelry Shelf   122

Index   127

About the Author   128

Acknowledgments   128

Introduction

Welcome to the wonderful world of macramé—an addictive craft making a big comeback from the kitschy art of the 1970s. I have always been an artistic person with creativity running through my veins. Long before I was born, my mom made a large macramé lantern, and I have strong memories of it hanging in my childhood home. It wasn't my favorite style, but the craft stuck in my mind.

I can't remember a time that I wasn't painting, carving wood, or crocheting, but it wasn't until 2019 when I first started making macramé projects. My obsession with houseplants got the best of me and I needed new ways to display my plants. I knew macramé would be the perfect solution! I started with plant hangers and instantly became addicted! I loved that macramé can be crafted by simply making a series of knots—it's a meditative art with endless creative possibilities. My love soon led to creating wall hangings, shelves, and eventually a business.

Creating anything is a wonderful way to express who you are, so I knew I had to share my passion for macramé with the world. In this book, I will walk you through the tools and materials required and teach you all the knots and patterns you need to get started! From there, all you need to do is pick your project! From decorative plant hangers to practical items like plant hangers, fruit storage, and shelves, there is a project for everyone in this book. Whether you are just starting out or have worked with cord before, you will find the perfect piece to build your skills and add a bit of art to your home.

Learning the approachable art of macramé will let you use simple knots to transform cords into beautiful and functional art for every space.

Gallery

You can use the macramé knots and patterns in this book to create a variety of gorgeous pieces, including jewelry, coasters, ornaments, and more. Once you've mastered the knots and tried your hand at the projects I've provided, use this gallery of a few of my favorite creations to spark your own artistic adventure.

Oakley Wall Hanging

This beautiful piece consists of four sections using the same knot pattern. It makes a gorgeous statement above your headboard.

KNOTS AND PATTERNS USED: lark's head knot, square knot, diagonal double half hitch knot, double half hitch diamond with accent knot
SIMILAR PROJECTS:
Celeste Wall Hanging, Arvin Wall Shelf

Moon Bookmarks

Bookmarks don't always have to be slim. Save your page with one of your own creations and enjoy it every time you open your book!

KNOTS AND PATTERNS USED: lark's head knot, square knot, diagonal double half hitch knot, gathering knot, double half hitch diamond with accent knot
SIMILAR PROJECT: Celeste Wall Hanging

Butterfly Wall Hanging

You can tie cords into variations of standard patterns to create images like this utterly captivating beauty!

KNOTS AND PATTERNS USED: lark's head knot, square knot, double half hitch knot and diagonal double half hitch knot, decreasing alternating square knots, double half hitch leaf
SIMILAR PROJECT: Coralynn Wall Plant Hanger

Azzura Wall Hanging

Textured large wall hangings with layered hues create magnificent focal points. This piece is perfect for a large accent on a plain wall, or to hang above a headboard.

KNOTS AND PATTERNS USED: lark's head knot, square knot, diagonal double half hitch knot, double half hitch diamond with accent knot, half knot sinnet (spiral knot)
SIMILAR PROJECT: Arvin Wall Shelf

Mini Crystal Sphere
or Plant Hanger

Macramé plant hangers are not always just for your plants. Display a gorgeous crystal sphere to add unique and elegant style.

KNOTS AND PATTERNS USED: gathering knot, square knot, square knot sinnet
SIMILAR PROJECT: Ariah Plant Hanger

Birch Wall Hanging

This smaller wall hanging is a lovely way to bring the tones of nature into your home.

KNOTS AND PATTERNS USED: lark's head knot, square knot, diagonal double half hitch knot, double half hitch diamond with accent knot
SIMILAR PROJECT: Arvin Wall Shelf

Moon Phase Wall Hanging

Creating images within your work breathes vibrant life and color into your masterpieces!

KNOTS AND PATTERNS USED: lark's head knot, square knot, gathering knot, square knot sinnet
SIMILAR PROJECT: Mushroom Wall Hanging

Everest Wall Hanging

The simplicity of this wall hanging is the true beauty of this piece. You can display a crystal in the center as I have, or let just the macramé speak for itself.

KNOTS AND PATTERNS USED: lark's head knot, double half hitch knot, half knot sinnet (spiral knot)

Macramé Garland

Working a macramé garland into your plant shelf, bookshelf, or mantel arrangements can truly elevate your decor.

KNOTS AND PATTERNS USED: lark's head knot, square knot, diagonal double half hitch knot, decreasing alternating square knots
SIMILAR PROJECT: Coralynn Wall Plant Hanger

Twyla Plant Hanger

Incorporate additional colors into your sinnets and get creative with how you use your plant holders. Disco balls add beautiful sparkle to a room.

KNOTS AND PATTERNS USED: gathering knot, half knot sinnet (spiral knot)
SIMILAR PROJECT: Ariah Plant Hanger

Aspen Plant Hanger

With this plant hanger, you can choose whether to hang it from the ceiling or against the wall. Either way, you can't go wrong.

KNOTS AND PATTERNS USED: lark's head knot, square knot, diagonal double half hitch knot, double half hitch diamond with accent knot, half knot sinnet (spiral knot)
SIMILAR PROJECTS: Celeste Wall Hanging, Stella Jewelry Shelf

Macramé Coasters

Macramé artistry can be simple, beautiful, and practical. Grab your cup of tea or coffee and protect (and decorate) your table with a macramé coaster!

KNOTS USED: lark's head knot, double half hitch knot

Sage Wall Hanging

Hung on a beautiful piece of driftwood and accented with a clear quartz crystal, this nature-inspired wall decor makes the perfect centerpiece in a living room or bedroom.

KNOTS AND PATTERNS USED: lark's head knot, square knot, diagonal double half hitch knot, double half hitch diamond with accent knot, alternating square knot, four-cluster square knot diamond
SIMILAR PROJECTS: Arvin Wall Shelf

Aura Feather Wall Hanging

Feather pieces bring so much character to a room, and playing around with different colors can really change the look and personality of a piece.

KNOTS USED: lark's head knot, reef knot, gathering knot
SIMILAR PROJECT:
Shiloh Feather Wall Hanging

Macramé Pumpkin

Macramé art meets holiday decor! A few simple knots come together to create delightful pieces to add to your festive autumn centerpieces

KNOTS AND PATTERNS USED: lark's head knot, square knot, gathering knot, square knot sinnet

Ember Wall Hanging

This stunning wall hanging is created with beautiful natural tones accented with dangling glass beads between each knot pattern. The light shining on the beads creates an elegant mix of colors.

KNOTS AND PATTERNS USED: lark's head knot, square knot, diagonal double half hitch knot, gathering knot
SIMILAR PROJECT: Celeste Wall Hanging

Feather Earrings

Wearing your own creations brings so much pleasure and joy to your life! Being asked "where did you get those?" and telling someone you made them is such a boost! I love the bohemian vibe these earrings add to any outfit.

KNOTS USED: reef knot
SIMILAR PROJECT: Shiloh Feather Wall Hanging

Macramé Angel

Creating these angels is a beautiful way to
honor a loved one. They also make perfect,
thoughtful gifts. Hang them as ornaments
during the holidays or display them all
year round.

KNOTS USED: overhand knot, gathering knot

Arden Wall Plant Hanger

When you're unable to hang anything from your ceiling, a wall plant hanger is the perfect solution.

KNOTS AND PATTERNS USED: lark's head knot, square knot, diagonal double half hitch knot, gathering knot, four-cluster square knot
SIMILAR PROJECTS: Haven Wall Cat Bed, Coralynn Wall Plant Hanger

Wall Hanging Hat Holder

This is a beautiful, unique way to display your favorite cowboy hats, garden hats, sun hats, etc. It's a fashionable piece with function.

KNOTS AND PATTERNS USED: lark's head knot, square knot, diagonal double half hitch knot, double half hitch diamond with accent knot
SIMILAR PROJECTS: Celeste Wall Hanging, Stella Jewelry Shelf

Macramé Mirror Frame

Use macramé to build a beautiful design around a metal ring, then add a simple circle mirror to enhance the beautiful and bohemian look!

KNOTS AND PATTERNS USED: lark's head knot, square knot, diagonal double half hitch knot, decreasing alternating square knot

Getting Started

Use macramé to add classic bohemian touches to your home.

So, you've decided you want to try your hand at macramé—great idea! Starting out can feel like the most difficult part of the journey, but I promise you it's easy! You're probably asking many questions: "What do I make?" "How much cord will I need?" "How do I make that knot?" "What supplies are best to use?" No worries, I am here to help! In this section, I first explain the basic tools and materials you will need to start any macramé project. In the sections that follow, you'll learn several basic macramé knots and how to use them together to create different styles, designs, and patterns. Finally, I've included a few tips and tricks to use along the way.

You'll need macramé cord, scissors, a measuring tape, and materials for hanging your macramé projects. Small wooden rings and beads are great decorative additions.

There are a few basic supplies you will need for every macramé project as well as some you can use to add extra character and personality. The basic tools are macramé cord, scissors, a wooden ring or dowel, and something from which to hang your working project. Other tools such as beads, crystals, and driftwood are all optional for creating unique pieces.

MACRAMÉ CORD—Macramé cord is the first thing you need. The most common cord type (and the type used for all projects in this book) is 3mm or 4mm 100% cotton cord. You will use either a single-strand cord or a 3- or 4-ply twisted cord (see below). Single-strand cords and twisted cords allow you to create different finishing looks, such as brushed-out single-strand tassels or unraveled 3-ply fringes. Ganxxet and Nook Theory are two of my favorite cord companies.

- *Single-strand cord* is the cord most often referred to as "macramé cord" and consists of one single strand.
- *Twisted cord* is often referred to as "rope" and consists of either three or four strands of rope twisted together (which is why they are referred to as 3-ply or 4-ply).

Cotton macramé cord gives the best results.

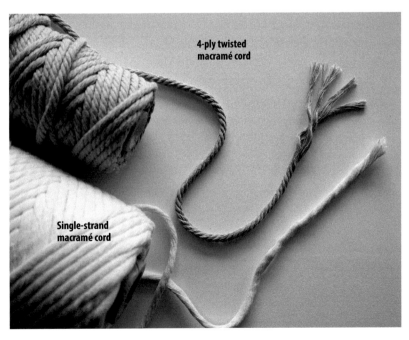

4-ply twisted macramé cord

Single-strand macramé cord

The type of cord you use will change the look and texture of your piece.

A quality clothing rack is the perfect base for working macramé.

CLOTHING RACK—Hanging your working project is necessary. I like to hang my work from a clothing rack using S hooks, which makes every piece much easier to work on. A clothing rack with wheels is even more useful, as you can easily move your working projects around as needed.

SCISSORS—A good pair of scissors is an important tool to have when it comes to macramé. You will do more cord cutting than you probably ever expected. My favorite pair of scissors are made by Gingher. If you plan to make macramé often, I suggest having multiple pairs of scissors.

TIP

Cutting your cord can be a tedious job. I recommend sliding a long dowel through the cord spool, then hanging each side of the dowel on a long S hook from your clothing rack. The cord will easily glide off the spool and ensure smooth, clean cuts.

You can also use a crate or basket with open handles, sliding the dowel with the cord spool on it through these handles to achieve a similar result.

SMALL RINGS—Rings are commonly used when making plant hangers and hanging baskets. You can use rings of any material, including wood or metal, just make sure they are durable enough to hold the weight of your project.

LARGE HOOPS—Hoops are used for various projects, including plant hangers and hanging baskets. They are most often made of wood, bamboo, or metal.

MEASURING TAPE—Your measuring tape will be your best friend! Use it with every project to measure the lengths of cord needed.

Add ornaments like wooden beads and rings in various sizes to enhance your knotting.

BEADS—Beads are a common accent to add to your macramé! Whether it be a plant hanger or a wall hanging, have fun with your options and choose the style, size, or color that fits your project!

Using driftwood or other found wood pieces in place of a plain dowel creates a more natural effect.

DRIFTWOOD OR DOWELS—Driftwood or any other hand-collected piece of wood is great to use when it comes to macramé. In this book, you will notice that I use driftwood for most of my wall hangings. I love using driftwood for my projects because it adds such a unique touch to each piece. The best part about using driftwood or any other type of found wood is that it is free! I collect all my wood pieces by hand and clean them before each use (see the tip below). Birchwood is also great for macramé. Or, you can use plain wooden dowels instead. Macramé cord is deceptively heavy, so be mindful when choosing a dowel or piece of wood. If you know you are making a larger piece that includes a large amount of cord, make sure to choose a thicker piece of wood to hang it from.

BRUSH OR COMB—A brush or comb is a useful tool for creating specific looks with the cord fibers. A few of the projects in this book require a brush or comb. A slicker pet brush is a great option for macramé—cord fibers often go everywhere when brushing out your macramé cord, but a slicker pet brush helps collect those loose fibers. You do not need a fancy brush; a simple comb will also do the job.

TIP

Clean your driftwood by first brushing away any loose pieces of dirt, then spraying it with water. Soak the driftwood in a mixture of water with a splash of bleach. Rinse the wood and allow it to dry completely.

Knot and Pattern Guide

In this section, you will learn the basic knots and patterns needed to create all the beautiful pieces in this book. In some of the step-by-step photos for the basic knots, I've included the cord numbers to help you get used to numbering the cords from left to right. Macramé knots are very forgiving; if you make a mistake, you can leave it as-is without dramatically affecting the finished piece or easily remove the knot and rework it. Unfortunately, if you notice a mistake that is far up in your work, you will have to unknot all the progress and rework it. That is the beauty of this craft, however! Mistakes happen, and you can easily fix them if you want or let them be unique quirks if you prefer.

Macramé is made by combining a variety of knots to create decorative patterns.

Common Terms and Abbreviations

In this book, you'll encounter a few terms that have specific meanings in the world of macramé. This book does not use the knot abbreviations, but I've included a short chart on page 27 of some you might encounter in other macramé patterns.

- **WORKING CORD(S):** These are the cords you are using to tie your knots. For example: when tying a square knot (see page 29), the two outside cords are your working cords.

- **FILLER CORD(S):**
  These are the center/inner cords around which you tie knots with your working cords. For example: when tying a square knot (see page 29), the two center cords are your filler cords.

- **UNRAVEL:**
  To untwist your cord. For example: untwisting a twisted 4-ply cord into four pieces (see Unraveling Twisted Cords on page 45).

- **SINNET:**
  A series of repeated knots. For example, multiple square knots in a row would be called a square knot sinnet.

Common Knot Abbreviations

LHK
Lark's head knot

RLHK
Reverse lark's head knot

SK
Square knot

HK
Half knot

RHK
Right-facing half knot

LHK
Left-facing half knot

DHHK
Double half hitch knot (aka clove hitch knot)

DDHHK
Diagonal
double half hitch knot

HHK
Half hitch knot

GK
Gathering knot
(aka wrap knot)

Lark's Head Knot

This knot is used to attach your cord to a piece of wood, ring, or another piece of cord. This knot is mostly used when starting your macramé piece.

Fold your cord in half and bring the top loop over the top of your dowel and to the back. Reach through the back of the loop and bring the two ends of cord through the loop.

Pull the ends of your cord to tighten.

TIP

When working with a lot of cord that you need to attach to your piece, form the knot in your hand and then slip the dowel through the loops. Forming the knot in this way, it will look like a pretzel at first. You'll fold the pretzel wings back to create the loop that slips onto the dowel.

Reverse Lark's Head Knot

Fold your cord in half and bring the top loop under your dowel and toward the front. Bring the two ends of the cord through the loop.

Pull the ends of your cord to tighten.

Half Knot

Whether made left-facing or right-facing, this knot typically is used with another knot following it, as it can come undone easily if used as a standalone knot.

Bring cord 1 over the filler cords (cords 2 and 3) and under cord 4. Bring cord 4 under the filler cords and through the loop created by cord 1.

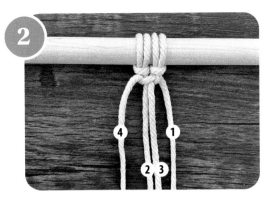

Pull cords 1 and 4 to tighten.

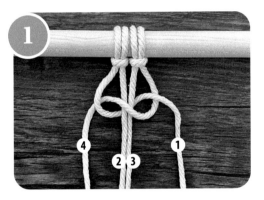

Bring cord 4 over the filler cords (cords 2 and 3) and under cord 1. Bring cord 1 under the filler cords and through the loop created by cord 4.

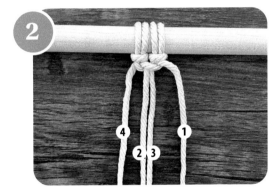

Pull cords 1 and 4 to tighten.

TIP

For all knots and patterns, you count your cords from left to right. Cord 1 is the first cord (on the left). In this example, cord 4 is the last cord (on the right).

Square Knot

This knot is one of the most common knots used in macramé. As you work through the projects, you will notice that I only tie right-facing square knots. You can use left-facing square knots if you prefer without changing the length of cord required.

Begin with a left-facing half knot (this will be the first half of your left-facing square knot).

Bring cord 4 over the two filler cords (cords 2 and 3) and under cord 1. Bring cord 1 under the filler cords and through the loop created by cord 4.

Pull cords 1 and 4 to tighten.

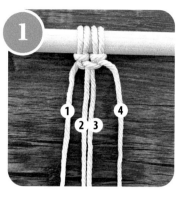

Begin with a right-facing half knot (this will be the first half of your right-facing square knot).

Bring cord 1 over the two filler cords (cords 2 and 3) and under cord 4. Bring cord 4 under the filler cords and through the loop created by cord 1.

Pull cords 1 and 4 to tighten.

This is a square knot variation in which you switch your working cords and filler cords.

Bring the outside working cords over the filler cords to the center so that the working cords become the filler cords and the filler cords become the working cords.

Tie a square knot with the new working cords.

Double Half Hitch Knot (aka Clove Hitch Knot)

This knot is used to create a variety of designs ranging from simple *V* shapes to leaf patterns. This knot is versatile and can be used to make horizontal or diagonal patterns.

Hold filler cord 1 horizontally or diagonally depending on the direction in which you want to work. Place working cord 2 behind the filler cord.

Bring cord 2 up and over cord 1, then over itself to the left, through the opening between cords 1 and 2.

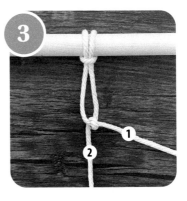

Pull the cords tight to create a half hitch knot.

TIP

Your direction will be determined by the direction in which you hold your filler cord. If you want your knots to go diagonal, hold your filler cord on a diagonal. If you want your knots to go horizontal, hold your filler cord horizontal.

Repeat steps 1–3 with the same working cord. The parts of the knot should be right next to each other.

Pull the cords tight to complete the double half hitch knot.

Reef Knot

This knot is a basic knot commonly used when making macramé feathers and leaves. It technically forms a "square knot," but it is different from the traditional macramé square knot.

Fold one cord in half, forming a loop.

Fold the second cord in half, forming another loop. Thread this loop through the first loop.

Bring the two end cords from the first loop over the second loop.

Pull both sets of cords tight to create the reef knot.

Gathering Knot (aka Wrap Knot)

This knot is often used to secure your cord together on plant hangers. It can be used to secure tassels, as well.

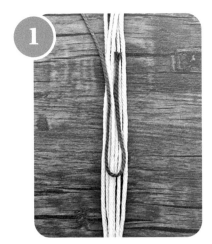

Fold a long working cord against your filler cords, creating a loop at the bottom that is around 3" (7.6cm) long and leaving a longer tail at the top for your wrapping. (The length of the bottom loop depends on how long you want your gathering knot to be.)

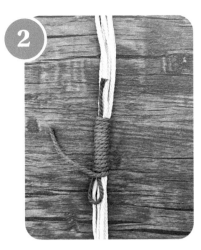

Use the longer tail end of the working cord to wrap around the looped shorter tail and all of your filler cords. Leave a small amount of the shorter tail end sticking out of the top. Wrap your long end all the way down until you have a small loop left.

Take the bottom tail end of your working cord and thread it through the loop on the bottom.

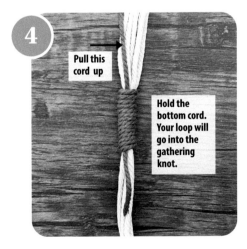

While holding the bottom cord, pull the top cord up. This will tighten your loop and will fit the loop inside your gathering knot.

Use your scissors to trim the top and bottom cords. Use your scissors to tuck the trimmed cords deeper into the knot.

Overhand Knot

This is a basic knot to help secure your work. It can be tied around a ring or around other cords.

Take one end of your cord and pull it around itself and through the loop it forms. (It will look like a pretzel.)

Pull both ends of the cord tight.

Making Tassels

Tassels can be fun to add to your wall hangings. Scrap cord is a great option to use when making your tassels.

Brush out your macramé cord. Take a longer cord and tie an overhand knot in the center of the brushed cord.

Using the same cord you tied around the brushed cord, tie an overhand knot around 2" (5.1cm) away from the first knot to create the hanging loop. Bring all the brushed cord together and use another cord to tie a gathering knot around it, about ½" (1.3cm) below the center point.

Constrictor Knot

The constrictor knot is the perfect knot to make when creating your hanging cord. One thing about this knot is that the tighter you pull the ends, the tighter your knot gets, and the more secure your cord is for hanging your final piece. This knot is perfect for heavy pieces.

1 Measure out the length you want for your hanging cord, adding approximately 8–10" (20.3–25.4cm) of extra length on each end for tying the knot. When tying this knot, you will want to work on the back of your piece.

2

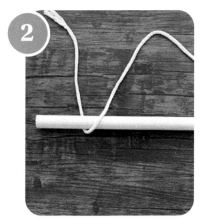

Starting on the left side, take the tail end of your cord and wrap it underneath and around the front of your dowel or wood piece.

3

Bring the tail end to the right and down across the cord to form an *X*.

4

Wrap the tail end under the dowel on the right. Bring the tail end over your hanging cord to the left.

5

Pull the end of your cord through the top of the x and out the bottom

Thread the tail end of your cord underneath the *X* and pull tight with both ends of the cord.

6 Repeat on the right side to finish your hanging cord, working your tail cord in the opposite direction.

Square Knot with Multiple Filler Cords

This knot is a great accent knot for macramé wall hangings. It changes the look drastically compared to a regular square knot.

Follow the steps for either the right-facing or left-facing square knot (see page 30) but increase the number of filler cords. When tightening your knot, make sure you align the cords so they are side by side and lay flat.

Square Knot with Multiple Working Cords

This knot also makes a nice accent knot in your project.

Follow the steps for either the right-facing or left-facing square knot (see page 30) but increase the number of working cords. You will have more than one working cord on each side. **NOTE:** I've also used multiple filler cords here. Adjust the cords so that they lie flat and do not overlap each other.

Square Knot Sinnet

This pattern is often used when making plant hangers and wall hangings. You can use right-facing or left-facing square knots.

Start by tying a square knot (see page 29)

Repeat to your desired length, tying square knots down the same filler cords with the same working cords. Make sure you keep your square knots tight and consistent. If you are tying a right-facing square knot, make sure to maintain the right-facing pattern. Do not switch directions or your cords will start to twist.

Half Knot Sinnet (aka Spiral Knot)

This is another pattern that is very common in plant hangers and wall hangings. You can use right-facing or left-facing half knots. Using right-facing half knots will create a left-twisting sinnet. Using left-facing half knots will create a right-twisting sinnet.

Start by tying a half knot (see page 29).

Repeat to your desired length, tying half knots down the same filler cords with the same working cords to create a spiral. Make sure you keep your half knots tight and consistent. If you are tying right-facing half knots, make sure to maintain the right-facing pattern.

Four-Cluster Square Knot Diamond

This pattern creates an elegant look in any piece and is particularly useful in wall hanging shelf designs.

Using the four cords in the middle, tie a square knot.

Using the first four cords, tie an alternating square knot, then repeat with the last four cords.

Using the four cords in the middle, tie a decreasing alternating square knot.

Alternating Square Knot

This pattern is common in creating wall hangings. You can play around with the design by creating the alternating square knot in increasing or decreasing patterns.

Tie square knots across the first row, using four cords for each square knot. I started with three square knots in this example.

Leaving out the first two cords, tie a square knot with the next four cords. You will use two cords from the first square knot and two cords from the second square knot. Repeat with the next four cords. Work across the row, leaving out the last two cords.

To continue the standard pattern, repeat steps 1 and 2 until you have reached the length you desire.

To finish as a decrease, leave out the first four cords and tie a square knot using the next four cords. In this example, I used two cords each from the previous two square knots in row 2. Work across the row, leaving out the last four cords. Repeat the process until you are left with a row of only one square knot.

Double Half Hitch Diamond with Accent Knot

This pattern is such a beautiful pattern to add a nice look to any piece. You can choose to only make the diamond and leave the center empty or add an accent knot to the center such as a square knot, weave pattern, or even a bead.

Start by tying a square knot using the four center cords. Cords 4 and 7 are the working cords and cords 5 and 6 are the filler cords.

Using cord 10 on the far right as your filler cord, tie four diagonal double half hitch knots, working from right to left. Using cord 1 on the far left as your filler cord, tie five diagonal double half hitch knots, working from left to right to close the point.

Using cord 1 as the filler cord, tie four more diagonal double half hitch knots, working from left to right. Using cord 10 as the filler cord, tie four more diagonal double half hitch knots, working from right to left.

Repeat steps 1–3 until you reach the desired length.

TIP

Instead of adding the square knot accent to the center of your diamond pattern, try adding a bead. When adding a bead, make sure that the interior diameter of the hole is big enough to thread the cords through. Use a beading tool (these work much like a needle threader) or tape the ends of your cords to make it easier to thread the cords through the bead. Also see page 46.

Double Half Hitch Leaf

Adding leaf patterns can change up the flow of your piece and give it some character. This is a relaxing pattern that's easy to create and looks beautiful.

Using cord 8 as your filler cord, tie seven diagonal double half hitch knots, working from right to left.

Using the farthest cord to the right as your filler cord, tie six diagonal double half hitch knots from right to left. Leave a slight gap between the first row and this row to create a more rounded, sloping angle. Your very first knot should be right against the first row, and the next five should be about ½" (1.3cm) below the first row.

Using the farthest cord on the left as your filler cord, tie seven diagonal double half hitch knots, working from left to right.

Using the farthest cord on the left as your filler cord, tie six diagonal double half hitch knots, working from left to right. Leave a slight gap between the first row and this row to create a more rounded, sloping angle. Your very first knot should be right against the first row, and the next five should be about ½" (1.3cm) below the first row. Finish the leaf shape, using the farthest cord on the right as the filler cord, by tying one double half hitch knot, working from right to left.

Zigzag

This is an easy pattern that allows you to play around to create versatile effects. You use the same filler cord throughout the entire pattern.

Using the farthest cord on the right as your filler cord and the next cord to its left as the working cord, tie seven diagonal double half hitch knots, working from right to left.

Using the same filler cord, tie seven diagonal double half hitch knots, working from left to right.

Repeat steps 1–2 until you reach the desired length.

Double Half Hitch Around a Ring or Dowel

You can easily use double half hitch knots to incorporate dowels or rings into your designs. When using this technique, the dowel or ring acts as the filler cord.

Starting with your first cord and using the dowel or ring as the filler, tie a standard double half hitch knot.

Continue tying double half hitch knots across the row.

Continuous Lark's Head Knots Around a Ring

Wrapping a ring with lark's head knots and reverse lark's head knots creates a clean finish. You can wrap rings of all sizes.

Tie an overhand knot around the ring, leaving a tail to become your hanging cord and bundling the working cord to keep it organized.

Bring the working cord under the ring, leaving a loop on the opposite side to the bundle.

Bring the working cord over the top of the ring, and through the loop to the right (A). Pull the bundled cord to tighten the lark's head knot (B).

Bring the working cord over the top of your ring, leaving a loop on the opposite side to the bundle. **NOTE:** Any time your last knot has the cord looped over the top (see where my finger is pointing in the photo), you will begin the next knot by going over your ring with the working cord.

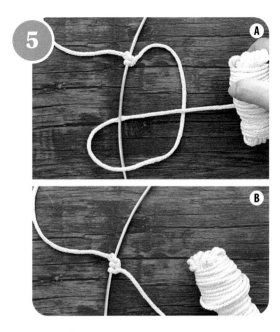

Bring the working cord under the ring and through the loop to the right (A). Pull the bundled cord tight to tighten the reverse lark's head knot (B).

Bring the working cord under your ring, leaving a loop on the opposite side to the bundle. **NOTE:** Any time your last knot has the cord looped underneath (see where my finger is pointing in the photo), you will begin the next knot by going under your ring with the working cord.

Repeat steps 3–6 to create continuous lark's head knots around your ring, making sure to adjust your knots as you go to keep them tight next to each other.

When you reach the end, use the end of the working cord and the tail you left out in step 1 to tie an overhand knot and finish the hanging cord.

Tips And Tricks

Who doesn't love a few good tips and tricks when it comes to creating! In this section, you will learn some quick fixes and special techniques. You'll also learn about a few additional tools and the best ways to keep them clean.

Be Consistent

The first important tip that I always tell beginner macramé artists is to make sure to keep consistent tension while tying your knots. This will keep your knots even and your finished work will look sharp and clean. If you tie your knots tight on one side of your piece and loose on the other, your work will not come out even and that can become frustrating.

Fixing a Mistake

The nice thing about macramé is that it's very forgiving. If you make a mistake, you can either untie your knots and start again or accept the flaw and move on with your piece. Sometimes a mistake is so minor you don't even notice it once your final piece is finished.

Helpful Tools

One thing you will notice when working with macramé cord is that the ends can fray easily. To prevent this from happening, tape the ends of your cord while working on your piece. Taping the ends also helps you more easily thread cords through when adding beads to your work. Tapestry needles or beading tools that work like needle threaders also help make beading a bit quicker and easier.

Keeping Your Macramé Clean

Believe it or not, a standard lint roller is the best tool for cleaning your macramé work. Roll it over your cord to lift any dust that has settled on your piece.

How Much Cord Do You Need?

Every time you start a project, you'll ask this question. Unfortunately, there is no solid answer. The length of cord you need will vary based on the complexity of your piece, the spacing and tension of your work, and the thickness of your cord. It is best to estimate the length of cords needed for your current project based on the length of cord you used for similar projects in the past. It is very helpful to write down the lengths you cut for any new projects you make so you can reference that information for all future projects. As you continue to work, you will begin to get a sense of the cord lengths you need to cut.

When starting out, though, a good rule for most standard projects, such as plant hangers and traditional knot patterns, is to cut your cord 4–6 times the length you want your finished piece to be. For example, if you want your plant hanger to finish around 20" (51cm) using several spiral knots or square knots, then you would want to cut your cord approximately 100" (254cm) long.

Avoid snags when unravelling twisted cords by starting at the bottom and working your way up.

Unraveling Twisted Cords

Unravelling twisted macramé cords can be time-consuming, but I promise the finished effect is always worth it! One way to avoid any snags when unraveling your cord is to start at the very bottom and twist the cords in the opposite direction to how they are twisted, then run your fingers through to help the process. Unraveling your cord will give you a beautiful wavy look. You can also use a comb or brush to brush the cord out—this removes the wavy look and creates more of a straight "fluffy" appearance.

Leftover Cord

What should you do with the leftover cord you cut from projects? Save it! Scrap cord can be very useful for future projects. Use it to add a fringe to your next piece or to make some fun tassels. One thing I love to use my scrap cord for is making decorative feathers. You can use tiny scraps to create feather earrings and larger scraps for feather wall hangings.

Adding Beads

Adding a bead to your work can help change the style and elevate your piece. For example, using a bead as an accent in a diamond pattern instead of a square knot creates a completely different look (see page 39). When adding a bead, make sure that the interior diameter of the hole is large enough to thread your macramé cord through. I like to use a beading tool (I use an EZ Beader) to help thread my cord through, but you can also use a needle with a large eye, like a tapestry needle, or even a bobby pin.

Thread the center cords through your bead and between your knots.

Secure your bead by finishing whichever pattern you are using. For example, I am tying a double half hitch diamond pattern with an accent bead.

Wall Hangings

Macramé wall hangings naturally enhance any space in your home.

Celeste Wall Hanging

This beautiful piece is not your average macramé wall hanging. This design consists of repeating sections of square knots and diamond, leaf, and zigzag patterns to create a stunning finished piece. What is most fun about it is how you can combine a variety of colors to add a unique look to your home decor!

This wall hanging uses symmetry and neutral colors to let the knotting shine.

Materials

- 240' (73.2m) of 4mm 4-ply twisted cotton macramé cord in your chosen colors (*I used Nook Theory colors cream, eucalyptus, and caramel*)
- 18" x 1" (45.7 x 2.5cm) piece of driftwood

Knots/Patterns Used

- Lark's head knot
- Square knot
- Diagonal double half hitch knot: diamond, leaf, and zigzag patterns
- Half knot sinnet (spiral knot)
- Gathering knot

Instructions

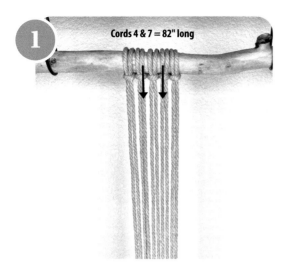

Cords 4 & 7 = 82" long

Cut five cords to 152" (386.1cm). Use lark's head knots to tie them in the center of your wood piece, leaving 8" (20.3cm) of wood on each side of the cords. Tie the first, third, and fifth lengths evenly; tie the second and fourth lengths so that cords 4 and 7 are 82" (208.3cm) long and cords 3 and 8 are 70" (177.8cm) long.

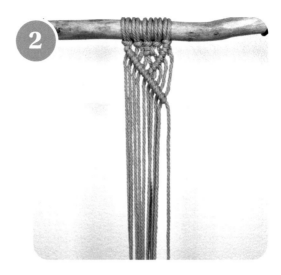

Using cords 4 and 7, tie a square knot around filler cords 5 and 6. Using cord 10 as your filler cord, tie four diagonal double half hitch knots to the left. Using cord 1 as your filler cord, tie nine diagonal double half hitch knots to the right.

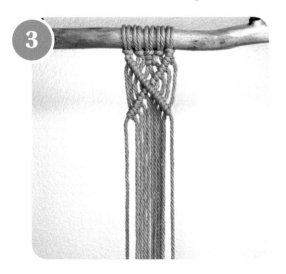

Using the fifth cord in (this cord was filler cord 10 from the previous step), tie four diagonal double half hitch knots to the left to create an *X* shape.

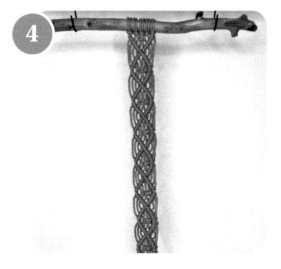

Repeat steps 2 and 3 to create seven full diamonds. Tie the filler square knots ½" (1.3cm) below the center of each *X*. On your last diamond, tie only five diagonal double half hitch knots to the right to close the point. Cut one cord to 24" (61cm) and use it to tie a gathering knot of at least six wraps around all the cords just below your last diamond to secure the knots. Trim the cords to 4" (10.2cm) long.

TIP

Cords 4 and 7 need to be longer as they will be the working cords for the accent knot in the diamond.

5

Cut two cords to 128" (325.1cm) and use lark's head knots to attach them 1" (2.5cm) to the right of the diamond pattern. Tie them so the filler cords are 23" (58.4cm) long and the working cords are 97" (2.5m) long. Tie ninety half knots to create a spiral that is 17" (43.2cm) long. Cut one cord to 20" (50.8cm) and use it to tie a gathering knot of at least six wraps around all the cords to secure the knots. Trim the cords to 4" (10.2cm). Repeat to the left of the diamond pattern.

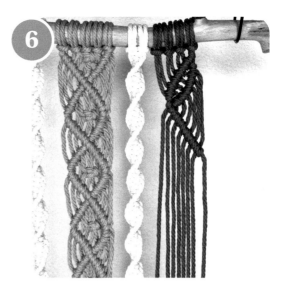

6

Cut four cords to 128" (325.1cm). Use lark's head knots to attach them evenly ½" (1.3cm) to the right side of the spiral knot. Using the far-right cord (cord 8) as your filler cord, tie seven diagonal double half hitch knots to the left. The space between your lark's head knot and final diagonal double half hitch knot should be 2" (5.1cm). Using the last cord as your filler cord, tie six diagonal double half hitch knots to the left, gradually increasing the amount of space between your knots to create a slope. Using the far-left cord (cord 1) as your filler cord, tie seven diagonal double half hitch knots to the right. This closes the leaf and starts the next one.

7

Using the far-left cord as your filler cord, tie six diagonal double half hitch knots to the right, gradually increasing the amount of space between your knots to create a slope.

8

Repeat the leaf pattern to create five more leaves. On your last leaf, tie only one diagonal double half hitch knot to the right to close the leaf. You should have a total of seven leaves. Trim the cords 4" (10.2cm) below the bottom leaf point.

Cut four cords to 128" (325.1cm). Use lark's head knots to attach them evenly ½" (1.3cm) to the left side of the spiral knot. Using the far-left cord (cord 1) as your filler cord, tie seven diagonal double half hitch knots to the right. The space between your lark's head knot and final diagonal double half hitch knot should be 2" (5.1cm). Using the first cord as your filler cord, tie six diagonal double half hitch knots to the right, gradually increasing the amount of space between your knots to create a slope.

Using the far-right cord as your filler cord, tie seven diagonal double half hitch knots to the left, then tie six diagonal double half hitch knots to the left, gradually increasing the amount of space between your knots to create a slope. Repeat the leaf pattern to create five more leaves. On your last leaf, tie only one diagonal double half hitch knot to the left to close the leaf. You should have a total of seven leaves. Trim the cords 4" (10.2cm) below the bottom leaf point.

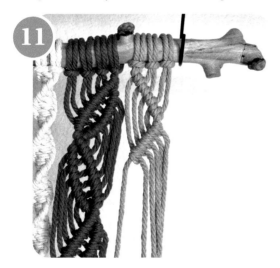

Cut two cords to 95" (241.3cm) and one cord to 82" (208.3cm). Using lark's head knots, attach the shorter cord ½" (1.3cm) to the right of the leaf pattern, leaving the outer filler cord at 32" (81.3cm) long and the inner working cord at 43" (109.2cm) long. Use lark's head knots to evenly attach the 95" (241.3cm) cords to the right of the 82" (208.3cm) cord. Using cord 1 as your filler cord, tie five diagonal double half hitch knots to the right. You should have 1½" (3.8cm) of space between your lark's head knot and the final diagonal double half hitch knot. Using the same filler cord, tie five diagonal double half hitch knots to the left. You should have 2" (5.1cm) of space between the rows along the left edge.

Repeat the zigzag pattern to create a total of nine zigzags. Trim the cords 4" (10.2cm) below the bottom zigzag point.

Cut two cords to 95" (241.3cm) and one cord to 82" (208.3cm). Using lark's head knots, attach the shorter cord ½" (1.3cm) to the left of the leaf pattern, leaving the outer filler cord at 32" (81.3cm) long and the inner working cord at 43" (109.2cm) long. Use lark's head knots to evenly attach the 95" (241.3cm) cords to the left of the 82" (208.3cm) cord. Using cord 6 as your filler cord, tie five diagonal double half hitch knots to the left. You should have 1½" (3.8cm) of space between your lark's head knot and the final diagonal double half hitch knot. Using the same filler cord, tie five diagonal double half hitch knots to the right. You should have 2" (5.1cm) of space between the rows along the right edge. Repeat the zigzag pattern to create a total of nine zigzags. Trim the cords 4" (10.2cm) below the bottom zigzag point.

Cut two cords to 100" (254cm). Using lark's head knots, attach them ½" (1.3cm) to the right of the zigzag pattern so that the inner filler cords are approximately 19" (48.3cm) long and the outer working cords are approximately 74" (188cm) long. Tie sixty half knots to create a spiral. Cut one cord to 20" (50.8cm) and use it to tie a gathering knot of at least six wraps around all the cords to secure the knots. Trim the cords to 4" (10.2cm). Repeat to the left of the zigzag pattern.

Untwist the cords at the bottom of each hanging section. Working from the outside edges in toward the centers, trim the cords at an angle. Tie a constrictor knot to create a hanging cord of the length you desire.

The driftwood adds a unique natural
touch to the finished piece.

This piece combines a wrapped ring with spiral knots to create a truly showstopping wall piece.

Tree of Life Wall Hanging

This is one of my all-time favorite pieces I've designed. It transforms one of the most common and approachable of macramé knots (the half knot sinnet/spiral knot) into a stunning bohemian tree. Hang it on the wall or from the ceiling and enjoy!

Materials

- 412' (125.6m) of 4mm 4-ply twisted cotton macramé cord in your chosen color *(I used AIFUN color natural)*
- 19" (48.3cm) metal hoop

Knots/Patterns Used

- Continuous lark's head knot (used to wrap the hoop)
- Lark's head knot
- Half knot sinnet (spiral knot)
- Gathering knot
- Overhand knot
- Square knot

Instructions

1

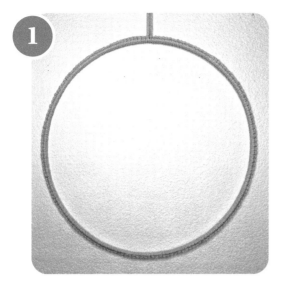

Cut one cord to 40' (12.2m). Tie an overhand knot around the metal hoop, leaving a 10" (25.4cm) tail on one side (this will become your hanging cord). Wrap your hoop, tying continuous lark's head knots and adjusting the knots tight to each other as you work. Twist the knots so they're on the outside of the hoop. Once you've wrapped all the way around, tie an overhand knot with the end of your wrapping cord to the 10" (25.4cm) tail you left at the beginning.

2

Cut eighteen cords to 13½' (4.1m), cut six cords to 15' (4.6m), and cut two cords to 19½' (5.9m). Set these cords aside.

TIP

Bundle your working cord to make it easier to wrap around your ring.

3

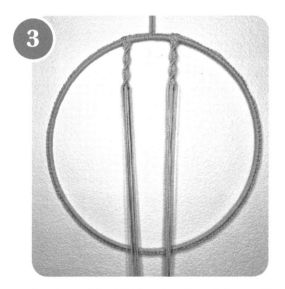

Attach two of the 13½' (4.1m) cords to the hoop with lark's head knots 2" (5.1cm) to the left of the hanging cord, leaving the center filler cords 60" (152.4cm) long, and the working cords 100" (254cm) long. Tie twenty half knots to create a spiral knot sinnet. This is branch 1. Repeat to the right of the hanging cord to create branch 2. for a total of 20 half knots creating a spiral knot.

4

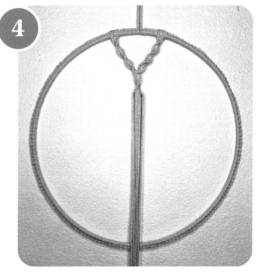

Combine branches 1 and 2 by using the working cords from branch 2 to tie ten half knots around all the cords to create a spiral knot sinnet.

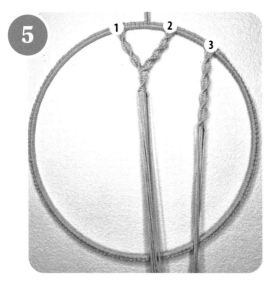

5

Use lark's head knots to attach the two 19½' (5.9m) cords to your hoop 3" (7.6cm) to the right of branch 2. Remember to keep your filler cords hanging to 60" (152.4cm) long. Tie thirty-five half knots to create a spiral knot sinnet.

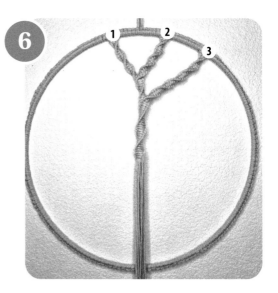

6

Use the working cords from branch 3 to tie twenty-six half knots around all the branch 1, 2, and 3 cords to create a spiral knot sinnet.

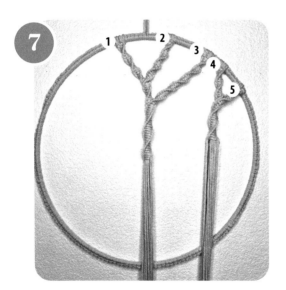

7

Attach two of the 13½' (4.1m) cords to the hoop with lark's head knots 1" (2.5cm) to the right of branch 3, leaving the filler cords 60" (152.4cm) long. Tie sixteen half knots to create a spiral knot sinnet. This is branch 4. Attach two more 13½' (4.1m) cords to the hoop with lark's head knots 2" (5.1cm) to the right of branch 4, leaving the filler cords 60" (152.4cm) long. Tie fourteen half knots to create a spiral knot sinnet. This is branch 5. Join branches 4 and 5 using the working cords from branch 5 to tie seventeen half knots around all the cords.

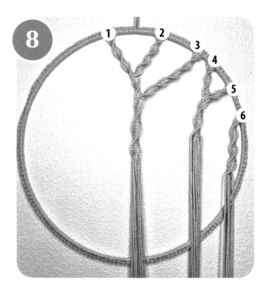

8

Attach two of the 13½' (4.1m) cords to the hoop with lark's head knots 2½" (6.4cm) to the right of branch 5, leaving the filler cords 60" (152.4cm) long. Tie twenty-eight half knots to create a spiral knot sinnet. This is branch 6.

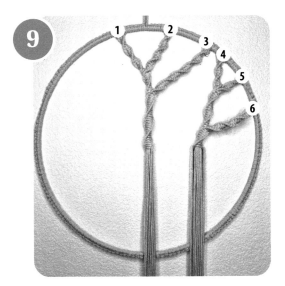

Use the working cords from branch 6 to tie ten half knots around all the branch 4, 5, and 6 cords to create a spiral knot sinnet.

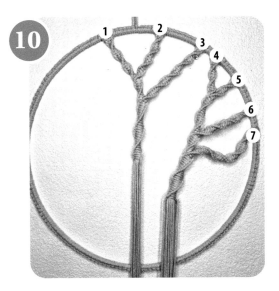

Attach two of the 15' (4.6m) cords to the hoop with lark's head knots 1" (2.5cm) to the right of branch 6, leaving the filler cords 60" (152.4cm) long. Tie thirty-eight half knots to create a spiral knot sinnet. This is branch 7. Use the working cords from branch 7 to tie twenty-two half knots around all the branch 4, 5, 6, and 7 cords to create a spiral knot sinnet.

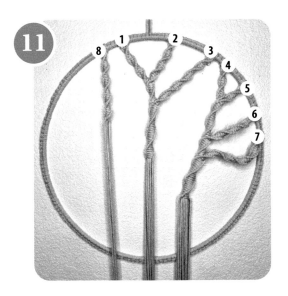

Attach two of the 15' (4.6m) cords to the hoop with lark's head knots 1" (2.5cm) to the left of branch 1, leaving the filler cords 60" (152.4cm) long. Tie thirty-two half knots to create a spiral knot sinnet. This is branch 8.

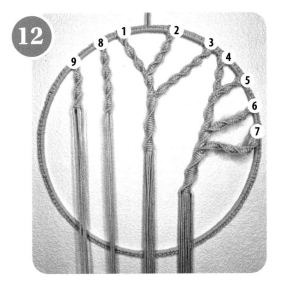

Attach two of the 13½' (4.1m) cords to the hoop with lark's head knots 2" (5.1cm) to the left of branch 8, leaving the filler cords 60" (152.4cm) long. Tie twenty half knots to create a spiral knot sinnet. This is branch 9.

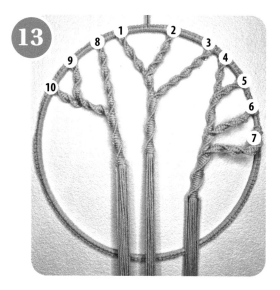

Attach two of the 13½' (4.1m) cords to the hoop with lark's head knots 2" (5.1cm) to the left of branch 9, leaving the filler cords 60" (152.4cm) long. Tie sixteen half knots to create a spiral knot sinnet. This is branch 10. Use the working cords from branch 9 to tie twelve half knots around all the branch 9 and 10 cords to create a spiral knot sinnet. Then, use the working cords from branch 8 to tie twenty-three half knots around all the branch 8, 9, and 10 cords to create a spiral knot sinnet.

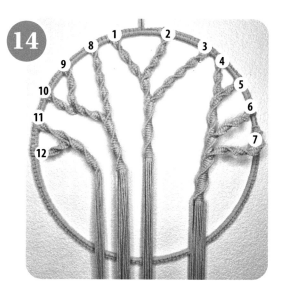

Attach two of the 15' (4.6m) cords to the hoop with lark's head knots 2" (5.1cm) to the left of branch 10, leaving the filler cords 60" (152.4cm) long. Tie sixteen half knots to create a spiral knot sinnet. This is branch 11. Attach two of the 13½' (4.1m) cords to the hoop with lark's head knots 2" (5.1cm) to the left of branch 11, leaving the filler cords 60" (152.4cm) long. Tie nineteen half knots to create a spiral knot sinnet. This is branch 12. Use the working cords from branch 11 to tie eighteen half knots around all the branch 11 and 12 cords to create a spiral knot sinnet.

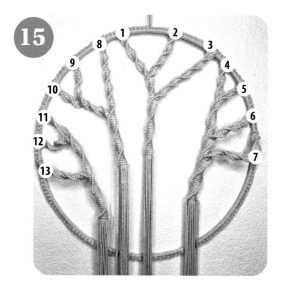

Attach two of the 13½' (4.1m) cords to the hoop with lark's head knots 1½" (3.8cm) to the left of branch 12, leaving the filler cords 60" (152.4cm) long. Tie twenty-six half knots to create a spiral knot sinnet. This is branch 13. Use the working cords from branch 11 to tie twenty-two half knots around all the branch 11, 12, and 13 cords to create a spiral knot sinnet.

Use the working cords from joined branches 1, 2, and 3 to tie ten half knots around all the cords from branches 1, 2, 3, 8, 9, and 10 to create a spiral knot sinnet.

Use the working cords from the center section to tie twenty half knots to create the final spiral knot sinnet.

Flip your work over and bring all the hanging cords to the back side of the hoop (the side closest to you). Starting with the working cords from your last spiral knot and working from opposite sides down toward the center, use overhand knots to attach all the cords to your hoop. Flip your work back around so it's facing forward.

Working in groups of four cords from left to right, tie thirteen square knots around the hoop.

Flip your work upside down. Measure approximately 10" (25.4cm) down from the bottom of the hoop and cut a straight line across the cords. This will ensure that the cords form a perfect *U* shape at the bottom.

This piece is stunning in a single neutral color, but you could also create it in color or add dye once you've finished knotting (see page 72).

TIP

Try turning your hoop as you're creating your side branches to make the knotting process easier.

Feathers are perfect starter macramé projects. In larger sizes and coordinating colors, they make great wall hangings.

Shiloh Feather Wall Hanging

Feathers have always been one of my favorite macramé pieces to make! They are beginner-friendly since they require only a couple knots and a simple brushed finish, and they instantly add so much character to your space. I mixed two coordinating colors, but you can completely change the look of this piece by using a single color or mixing in even more colors.

Materials

- 44' (13.4m) of 4mm 4-ply twisted cotton macramé cord in your chosen colors (*I used Nook Theory colors eucalyptus and cream*)
- 19" x 1" (48.3 x 2.5cm) piece of driftwood
- Tape
- Brush or comb
- Cardboard or paper (optional, used as background for spraying the fabric stiffener)
- Fabric stiffener (optional, used to hold the shape of the feathers)

Knots/Patterns Used

- Lark's head knot
- Reef knot
- Gathering knot
- Constrictor knot (used for hanging your piece)

Instructions

1

Cut two cords of both colors (four cords total) to 35" (89cm). These will be the filler cords (spine) of your feathers. Cut one hundred cords of both colors (two hundred cords total) to 6½" (16.5cm). These will be your working cords; set them to the side.

2

Fold the 35" (89cm) cords evenly in half and attach them to the driftwood with lark's head knots. Measure 1" (2.5cm) below the lark's head knots and tape your cords together. Remove the cords from the driftwood and set three aside.

3

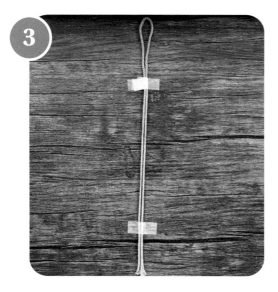

Starting with the first spine cord, tape the top onto your surface over the spot where the cord is taped together. Tape the bottom of the cord down, leaving 1½" (3.8cm) of cord at the bottom.

4

Using two of the 6½" (16.5cm) working cords in the same color, make a reef knot around the spine filler cord.

TIP

Tying and taping your cords in advance ensures that your feathers will fit the driftwood once they are made, while allowing you to more easily make them since they don't need to be attached to the wood.

Repeat step 4 until you've created twenty-five reef knots total.

Remove the tape from the bottom of your feather and brush out the extra cord all around the feather on the front and back. It's easiest to start at the ends of the cords and work your way in toward the spine.

TIP

The fabric stiffener is optional. Not spraying your feathers will leave you with a beautiful, fluffy finish.

Face the bottom of your feather away from you and begin cutting the shape of your feather. Work slowly and remember that you can always trim away more cord if needed.

Remove the remaining tape and relocate your feather to a piece of cardboard or paper. Generously spray your feather with the fabric stiffener and rub it in. Flip your feather and repeat on the other side. This will help hold the shape. Set your feather aside and allow it to dry.

9

Repeat steps 3 through 8 to create the three remaining feathers.

10

Attach the feathers to the driftwood by first forming a lark's head knot in your hand and then sliding the cord on, alternating the colors.

11

Cut two cords of both colors (four cords total) to 6" (15.2cm). Using matching cord colors, tie a gathering knot around each set of hanging cords just below the driftwood. Each gathering knot should be at least two wraps around.

12

Cut one cord to 40" (101.6cm) to become the hanging cord. Secure it onto your driftwood by tying constrictor knots 1" (2.5cm) in from each end. Hang your piece and enjoy its beauty!

Mixing natural colors allows you to bring
earthy elegance into your home.

TIP

*To make larger feathers, cut your spine cord longer
and add more reef knots. Try layering smaller
feathers to create more dimension.*

Macramé doesn't often involve color changes within knot patterns, but they create amazing results.

Mushroom Wall Hanging

If bohemian natural decor is your style, this unique design is perfect for you! This piece is not your average macramé, using multiple square knots and color changes to create a singular design. Choose your favorite color and let's get to work!

Materials

- 156½' (47.7m) 4mm single-strand cotton macramé cord in your chosen background color (*I used Ganxxet color moon*)
- 40⅓' (12.3m) 4mm single-strand cotton macramé cord in your chosen mushroom cap color (*I used Ganxxet colors ocher and red*)
- 14' (4.3m) 4mm single-strand cotton macramé cord in your chosen mushroom stem color (*I used Ganxxet color chestnut*)
- 13" x 1" (33 x 2.5cm) piece of driftwood

Knots/Patterns Used

- Lark's head knot
- Square knot sinnet
- Gathering knot

Instructions

1

Cut twenty cords of the background color to 42" (106.7cm) and attach them evenly to your driftwood with lark's head knots.

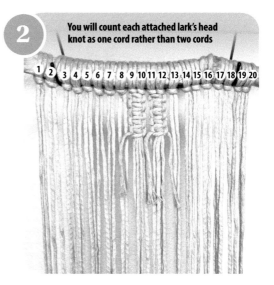

2

You will count each attached lark's head knot as one cord rather than two cords

1 2 3 4 5 6 7 8 9 10 11 12 13 14 15 16 17 18 19 20

Cut two background color cords to 28" (71.1cm) and use them to tie five square knots around cords 9 and 10 (to create column 5) and cords 11 and 12 (to create column 6).

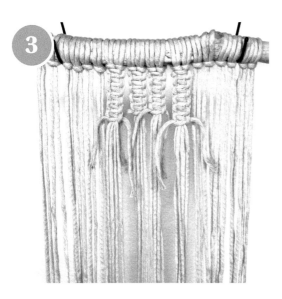

3

Cut two background color cords to 32" (81.3cm) and use them to tie six square knots around cords 7 and 8 (to create column 4) and cords 13 and 14 (to create column 7).

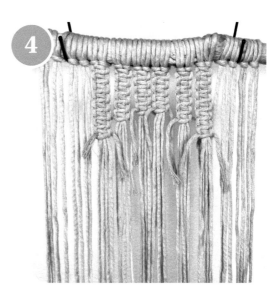

4

Cut two background color cords to 40" (101.6cm) and use them to tie eight square knots around cords 5 and 6 (to create column 3) and cords 15 and 16 (to create column 8).

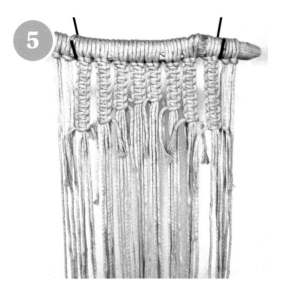

5

Cut two background color cords to 46" (116.8cm) and use them to tie nine square knots around cords 3 and 4 (to create column 2) and cords 17 and 18 (to create column 9).

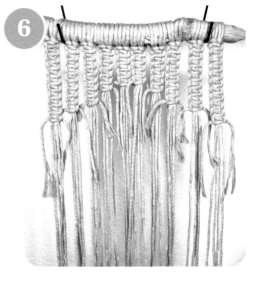

6

Cut two background color cords to 56" (142.2cm) and use them to tie eleven square knots around cords 1 and 2 (to create column 1) and cords 19 and 20 (to create column 10).

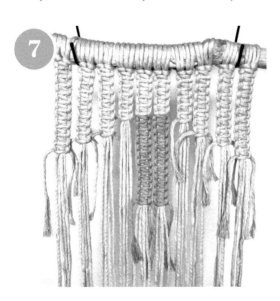

7

Cut two mushroom cap color cords to 60" (152.4cm) and use them to tie twelve square knots in columns 5 and 6, working right below your background color square knot sinnets. See the Tip at right for more details on color changes.

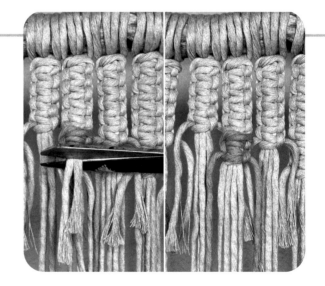

Tie two square knots in the new color around the working cords and filler cords of the previous color, then cut the previous color working cords on the back of the piece.

This is how the color change will look after the previous color working cords are cut. Flip the piece back over and complete the remaining knots.

TIP

When changing colors, you tie the first two square knots over the working cords and filler cords of the previous color. Then, you cut the working cords in the back of your piece. (This is the process every time you change your cord color.)

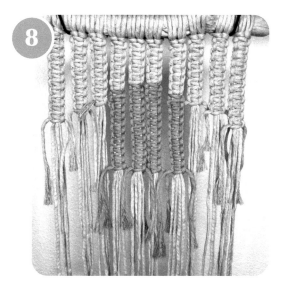

8

Cut two mushroom cap color cords to 56" (142.2cm) and use them to tie eleven square knots in columns 4 and 7, working right below your background color square knot sinnets.

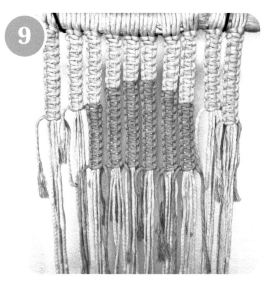

9

Cut two mushroom cap color cords to 52" (132.1cm) and use them to tie nine square knots in columns 3 and 8, working right below your background color square knot sinnets.

10

Cut two mushroom cap color cords to 42" (106.7cm) and use them to tie eight square knots in columns 2 and 9, working right below your background color square knot sinnets.

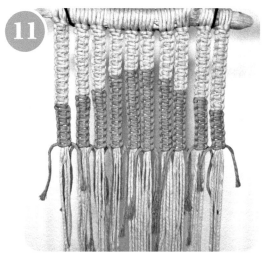

11

Cut two mushroom cap color cords to 32" (81.3cm) and use them to tie six square knots in columns 1 and 10, working right below your background color square knot sinnets.

Cut four mushroom stem color cords to 42" (106.7cm) and use them to tie eight square knots in columns 4, 5, 6, and 7, working right below the mushroom cap color square knot sinnets.

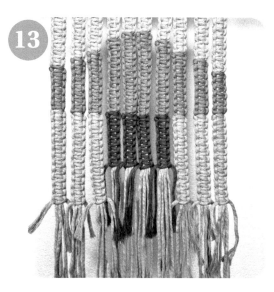

Cut six background color cords to 62" (157.5 cm) and use them tie thirteen square knots in columns 1, 2, 3, 8, 9, and 10, working right below the mushroom cap color square knot sinnets.

Cut four background color cords to 28" (71.1 cm) and use them to tie five square knots in columns 4, 5, 6, and 7, working right below the mushroom stem color square knot sinnets.

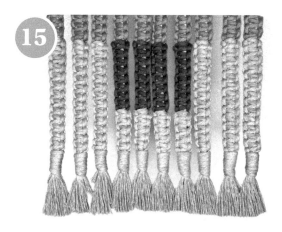

Cut ten background color cords to 15" (38.1cm) and use them to tie gathering knots of at least six wraps at the end of each column, just below the last square knot. Trim the bottoms to your liking and brush the fringe.

16

Use the cord color of your choice to tie a constrictor knot and create a hanging cord of the desired length.

Macramé cords are a nice alternative to a traditional canvas—you can use dyes to create truly unique art pieces.

Leo Mountain Dyed Wall Hanging

Dyed macramé pieces have become very popular, and I can see why! These pieces are so beautiful and let you add your own creative touch to them. Allow yourself to have fun with this piece and choose whichever color you love to create with! Transform your cords into any of your favorite gorgeous scenes.

Materials

- 240' (73.2m) of 4mm 3-ply twisted cotton macramé cord in your chosen color *(I used AIFUN color natural)*
- 24" x 2" x 1" (61 x 5.1 x 2.5cm) wood board
- Staple gun and ⁵⁄₁₆" staples
- Fabric dye in chosen color (I used Rit color charcoal grey)
- Dye fixative (I used Rit ColorStay Dye Fixative)
- Water
- Spray bottle
- Glass container for mixing
- Paintbrushes in multiple sizes
- 1½" (3.8cm) painter's tape
- Gloves
- Cardboard, packing paper, or canvas drop cloth (optional dyeing surface)

12½"
16½"
8"
10"
7"
5"
3"
12"
6"
6"
7"
5"
6"
5"
5½"
6½"
4"
6"
6½"

Fabric dye can be daunting, but as long as you work slowly to build your color saturation and protect your skin and work surface, it'll be a rewarding experience.

Wood Board

Painter's Tape

Macramé Cord

Spray Bottle And Water

WATER

Dye Fixative

Fabric Dye

Rit

charcoal grey
gris marengo

Rit
ColorStay
Dye Fixative
Fijador de Tinte
ColorStay

Glass Container (With Prepared Fabric Dye)

2 CUPS

Paintbrushes

Gloves

Cardboard, Packing Paper, Or Canvas Drop Cloth

Instructions

Cut forty-eight cords to 60" (152.4cm). On the back of the wood, measure 2" (5.1cm) in on each end and make a mark, then measure ½" (1.3cm) up from the bottom and draw a line between the two end marks. This is your baseline for attaching your cords.

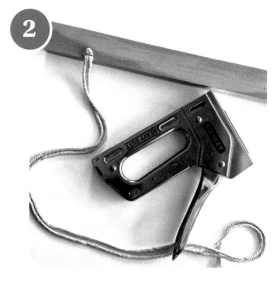

Fold your cords evenly in half. Place the top of the folded cord just below the measured line. Use your staple gun to staple the top of the cord to the wood.

Continue to staple the remaining cords right next to each other along the entire line. You should be able to fit all forty-eight cords within the 20" (50.8cm) space, but if you need more or fewer cords to fill the space, that is okay.

Place a flat piece of cardboard, packing paper, or canvas drop cloth on your work surface, making sure it's secure. Lay your macramé piece down on the work surface and arrange the cords so they are parallel and lie flat. Use the painter's tape to tape the cords to the table 3" (7.6cm) below the wood board and 3" (7.6cm) up from the bottom.

5

Starting on the left side of your piece, measure down 16½" (41.9cm). Begin placing a 6" (15.2cm) piece of painter's tape, starting on your work surface and angling it to end around 4" (10.2cm) up to the right. Place a second 6" (15.2cm) piece of painter's tape, starting on this peak and angling it to end around 4" (10.2cm) down to the right.

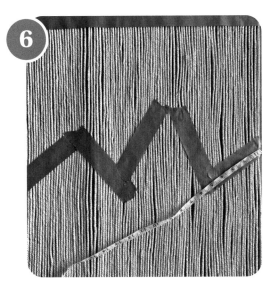

6

Place a third 6" (15.2cm) piece of painter's tape, starting slightly above the bottom of your first mountain and angling it to end around 3" (7.6cm) up to the right. Place a 7" (17.8cm) piece of painter's tape, starting on this peak and angling it to end around 3" (7.6cm) down to the right. Place a 5" (12.7cm) piece of painter's tape, starting slightly above the bottom of your second mountain and angling it to end on the work surface up to the right.

7

Create the two top mountain peaks using the same tape technique. These mountains are above the first peaks to the right and are just below the top tape line. Create the two mountain peaks along the bottom (not yet shown).

TIP

Refer to the taped and measured picture on page 73 periodically as you work. Remember, though, that your piece doesn't have to perfectly match mine!

8

Using a spray bottle filled with water, saturate all the cords below the taped mountain peaks. You want your cords to be really wet, so you may need to remove the spray nozzle as I have to add the water more directly.

Prepare the fabric dye in the glass container following the directions on the back of the package. Dip the end of a paintbrush in the dye and outline the lower edge of each taped mountain peak. Make short, downward brushstrokes. Be light-handed at first until you get the hang of it. You can always go back and make your strokes darker and thicker if needed.

Once you've finished dyeing the mountain peak outlines, use your paint brush to fill in the bottom mountains and the cord ends. Dye around the tape for now—you will remove it and fill this space later.

Remove the tape from the mountain peaks and fill in any gaps where the tape was overlapping. Touch up other spots as needed.

Remove the bottom tape line and saturate the entire bottom with dye.

13

Staple a piece of macramé cord to the back of the wood for hanging or add a sawtooth picture hanger if you want a piece with no hanging cord.

14

Hang your piece over a drop cloth to allow the bottom to drip dry. Your piece will dry much faster if you place a fan in front of it.

This technique creates a soft, elegant image that works equally well as a neutral backdrop or a centerpiece.

Haven Wall Cat Bed

This unique way to display your cat bed will have you and your cat loving everything about it! The steps explain how to create a spiral knot sinnet hanging cord as a sturdy, attractive option, but you can also tie constrictor knots and leave extra-long hanging cords at the sides with beads attached for a completely different effect (see the orange-colored variation).

This variation on the design uses a plain hanging cord with beads rather than a spiral knot cord.

Materials
- Approximately 434¾' (132.5m) of mm single-strand macramé cord in your chosen color
  (*I used Ganxxet colors berry red and apricot*)
- 18½" x 1" (47 x 2.5cm) dowel
- 16" (40.6cm) metal ring

Knots/Patterns Used
- Lark's head knot
- Square knot
- Double half hitch knot
- Square knot with multiple filler cords
- Square knot with multiple working cords
- Double half hitch knot around a ring or dowel
- Half knot sinnet (spiral knot)
- Reverse lark's head knot
- Gathering knot

Instructions

1

Cut twenty cords to 148" (375.9cm) and fold them evenly in half. Use lark's head knots to tie them around the dowel. The individual hanging cords are each counted, so your first lark's head knot creates cords 1 and 2, and so on.

2

Using cords 3 and 6, tie a square knot around cords 4 and 5. Using cord 7 as your working cord and cord 8 as your filler cord, tie three diagonal double half hitch knots to the left. Using cord 2 as your working cord and cord 1 as your filler cord, tie four diagonal double half hitch knots to the right.

3

Repeat step 2 four more times, working across your dowel to create a total of five half diamonds made with eight cords each.

4

Using cords 6 and 7 as the left working cords, cords 10 and 11 as the right working cords, and cords 8 and 9 as the filler cords, tie a square knot with multiple filler and working cords.

Repeat step 4 three more times, skipping two cords in between each square knot. You will have a total of four square knots made with six cords each.

Using cord 11 as your working cord and cord 12 as your filler cord, tie three diagonal double half hitch knots to the left. Using cord 6 as your working cord and cord 5 as your filler cord, tie four diagonal double half hitch knots to the right to close the point.

Repeat step 6 three more times, using groups of twelve cords to tie three diagonal double half hitch knots to the left and four diagonal double half hitch knots to the right to close the point. The second diamond uses cords 20 and 13 as filler cords, the third diamond uses cords 28 and 21 as filler cords, and the final diamond uses cords 36 and 29 as the filler cords.

Using the six cords between each diamond point, tie three square knots with multiple filler and working cords. **NOTE:** You will leave out the first and last nine cords.

9

Tie three diamond points, using groups of twelve cords to tie three diagonal double half hitch knots to the left and four diagonal double half hitch knots to the right to close the point. The first diamond uses cords 16 and 9 as filler cords, the second diamond uses cords 24 and 17 as filler cords, and the final diamond uses cords 32 and 25 as the filler cords.

10

Using the six cords between each diamond point, tie two square knots with multiple filler and working cords. **NOTE:** You will leave out the first and last thirteen cords.

11

Tie two diamond points, using groups of twelve cords to tie three diagonal double half hitch knots to the left and four diagonal double half hitch knots to the right to close the point. The first diamond uses cords 20 and 13 as filler cords and the second diamond uses cords 28 and 21.

12

Tie your last square knot with multiple filler and working cords using cords 18 through 23. Tie one diamond point, using the center twelve cords to tie three diagonal double half hitch knots to the left and four diagonal double half hitch knots to the right to close the point. The diamond uses cords 24 and 17 as filler cords.

13

Using cord 2 as your working cord and cord 1 as your filler cord, tie nineteen diagonal double half hitch knots to the right just below and tight to the diamonds. Using the second-to-last cord (cord 39) as your working cord and the last cord (cord 40) as your filler cord, tie twenty diagonal double half hitch knots to the left to close the point.

14

Using the first four cords, tie a square knot. Working in groups of four cords, tie four more square knots on the left side. Repeat on the right side, working in groups of four cords to tie five more square knots. Using two cords each from the two inner square knots, tie one center square knot.

15

Repeat step 13, leaving approximately 1" (2.5cm) of space below the square knots.

16

Using the first six cords on the left, tie a square knot with multiple filler and working cords, leaving approximately 2" (5.1cm) of space below the diagonal double half hitch knots. Repeat with the last six cords on the right. Using cord 8 as your working cord and cord 7 as your filler cord, tie thirteen diagonal double half hitch knots to the right. Repeat on the other side, using cord 33 as your working cord and cord 34 as your filler cord to tie fourteen diagonal double half hitch knots to the left to close the point.

17

Cut four cords to 90" (228.6cm) and use lark's head knots to attach two of them on the left side of your dowel, letting the filler cords hang to 18" (45.7cm). Tie sixty half knots to create a spiral knot sinnet. Repeat on the right side.

18

Cut six cords to 12" (30.5cm) and brush them out. Align them evenly between the two center filler cords of one of the spiral knot sinnets and use the working cord to tie two half knots to secure. Brush all the cords again. Cut one cord to 20" (50.8cm) and tie a gathering knot of at least six wraps ½ inch (1.3cm) down from the top of the brushed cord. Trim the tassel to 5" (12.7cm). Repeat on the other side.

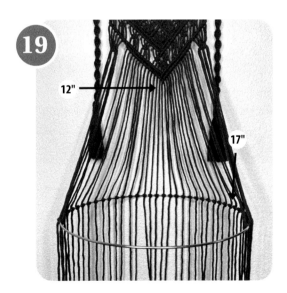

19

Attach the cords to the 16" (40.6cm) metal ring with lark's head knots, starting with the center cord and then the two outer cords to keep it stable. The first lark's head knot should be 12" (30.5cm) down on the center cord. The lark's head knots on the outer cords should be 17" (43.2cm) down. The space on each side between the center cord and the outer cords on the ring should be around 14" (35.5cm). Continue to tie lark's head knots with the remaining cords.

20

Cut twenty cords to 53" (134.6cm) and use reverse lark's head knots to attach them evenly to the front of the metal ring.

21

Cut one cord to 54" (137.2cm). Gather together all your hanging cords to create the basket and tie a gathering knot of at least ten wraps approximately 9" (22.9cm) down from metal ring. Your cat bed may hang slightly forward at this point, but once you hang it on the wall it will adjust itself.

22

Cut two cords to 180" (457.2cm) and use reverse lark's head knots to attach them to the left side of your dowel, letting the filler cords hang to 37" (94cm). Tie one hundred twenty half knots to create a spiral knot sinnet. Twist your spiral knot sinnet up over the top of the dowel and curved to the right side. Use the two working cords to tie a lark's head knot around the dowel, keeping your filler cords in the back of your piece.

23

Once the outside cords are secured to the dowel, use them to tie two overhand knots around the two filler cords to secure them tight on the back of your piece. Trim your cords and your bed is ready to display!

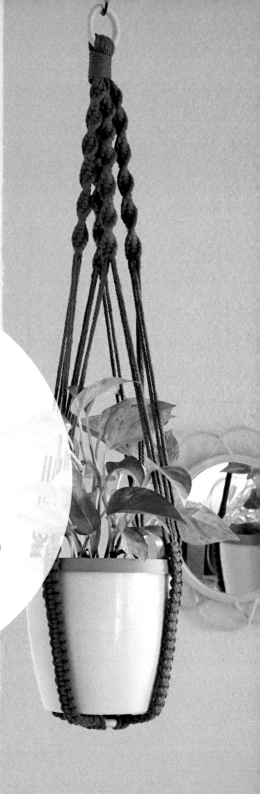

Plant Hangers

My macramé journey began with my love
of plants and my desire to find unique
means of displaying my greenery.

This plant hanger uses beautifully interlocked spirals to create a finish that complements any type of plant.

Ayla Plant Hanger

If you love plants as much as I do, you will love this plant hanger basket. The natural beauty of the cord against the bold green leaves makes this plant hanger a lovely choice! I use my Ayla plant hanger to display one of my gorgeous Pothos plants.

Materials

- Approximately 155' (47.2m) of 4mm single-strand macramé cord in your chosen color (*I used Ganxxet color natural*)
- Two 6" (15.2cm) bamboo hoops

Knots/Patterns Used

- Gathering knot
- Double half hitch knot
- Half knot sinnet (spiral knot)

Instructions

Start of gathering knot   **Halfway point**   **End of gathering knot**

Cut six cords to 120" (304.8cm) in length. Gather the cords together and fold them evenly in half to find the halfway point. Cut one piece of cord to 70" (177.8cm) and use it to tie a 4" (10.2cm) gathering knot around the six cords, starting 2" (5.1cm) to the left of the halfway point and ending 2" (5.1cm) to the right of the halfway point.

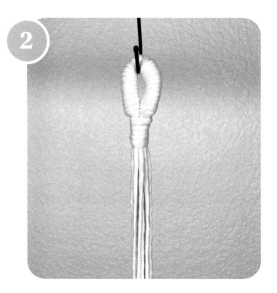

Cut one cord to 20" (50.8cm). Fold the six cords in half so that the ends of the 4" (10.2cm) gathering knot are aligned. Use the 20" (50.8cm) cord to tie a 1" (2.5cm) gathering knot of six wraps around the folded cords to create a hanging loop.

Divide the cords into three sections of four cords each. Measure 20" (50.8cm) down from the bottom of the gathering knot and use double half hitch knots to attach the cords to one of the bamboo hoops. Space each section around 5" (12.5cm) apart.

Cut twenty-four pieces of cord to 72" (182.9cm) in length. Use reverse lark's head knots to attach the cords to the hoop, leaving the filler cords hanging to 32" (81.3cm) long and the working cords hanging to 37" (94cm). Each section should have eight cords attached.

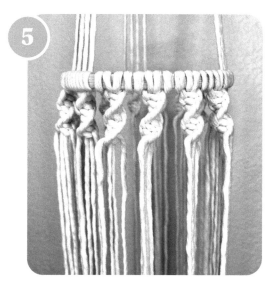

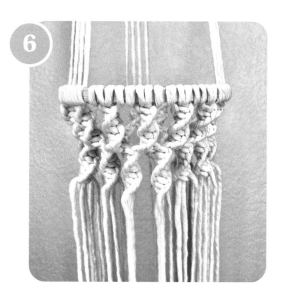

Starting with four cords from your first section connected in step 3, tie eight right-facing half knots to create a left-twisting sinnet that is about 1½" (3.8cm) long. Repeat with the remaining twenty cords, working in groups of four cords to create a total of fifteen left-twisting sinnets.

Alternate your working cords and your filler cords (using cords from two of the previous knots to create new knots) and tie eight right-facing half knots to create a left-twisting sinnet that is about 1½" (3.8cm) long. Repeat with the remaining twenty cords, working in groups of four cords to create a total of fifteen left-twisting sinnets.

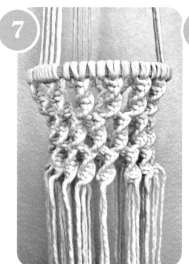

Repeat step 6 to create row 3.

Tie double half hitch knots to attach all thirty-six cords to the second bamboo hoop.

Cut one piece of cord to 40" (101.6cm). Gather all the strands of hanging cord as tight as possible to the bottom center of the basket and tie a gathering knot of at least ten wraps that is 1½" (3.8cm) long. Trim the remaining cords 6" (15.2cm) below the gathering knot.

This design creates a supportive flat base for your plants without the need for a wooden base.

Merek Plant Hanger

This plant hanger is named after my son, who helped provide a little inspiration and creativity while I was designing it. You may not always have rings or other tools available for starting your plant hanger—this design allows you to create and display your piece using only the cord you have on hand. Adding a wooden round to the base adds extra character and gives you the option of displaying other items like crystals, books, or even more plants.

This plant hanger can be used with or without a wooden round base to display plants or any other small items—making it a versatile piece you can use anywhere in your home.

Materials
- Approximately 131½' (334cm) of 4mm 4-ply twisted cotton macramé cord in your chosen colors (*I used Nook Theory color cream*)

- Painter's tape
- Wooden round (optional)

Knots/Patterns Used
- Square knot
- Half knot sinnet (spiral knot)
- Gathering knot

Instructions

1

Cut four cords to 11' (3.4m) long, cut two cords to 20' (6.1m) long, and cut two cords to 22' (6.7m) long.

2

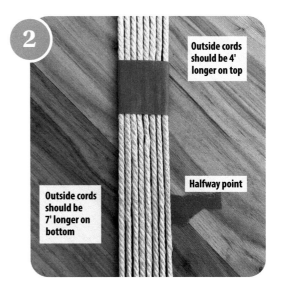

Outside cords should be 4' longer on top

Halfway point

Outside cords should be 7' longer on bottom

Lay the shortest cords on the floor parallel to each other, keeping the halfway points aligned. Lay each 20' (6.1m) cord on either side of the four central cords, aligning the halfway points so the cords extend 4½' (1.4m) past the center cords on the ends. Lay each of the longest cords on either side of the 20' (6.1m) cords so that the cords extend 4' (1.2m) past the center cords on the top and 7' (2.1m) past the center cords on the bottom. Place painter's tape around your cords 2" (5.1cm) up from the halfway point.

3

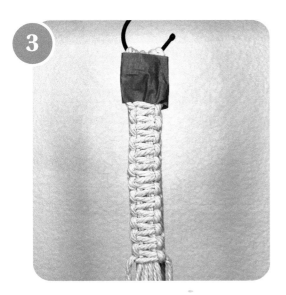

Using the two outside cords, tie twelve square knots starting right below the tape.

4

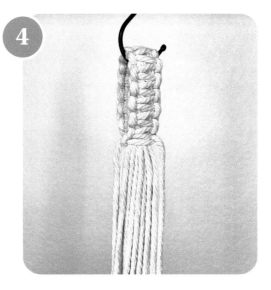

Fold the square knot sinnet evenly in half and tie two half knots to secure the hanging loop.

5 Divide the cords into four sections, each having two long cords and two short cords. Using two long cords, tie seventy-five half knots to create a spiral knot sinnet. Repeat with the other three sections.

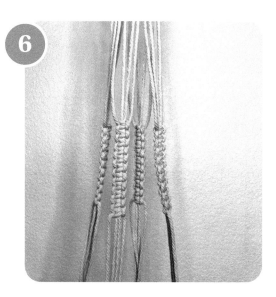

6 Alternate the cords so that you are using one working cord each from two separate sections as filler cords and one filler cord each from two separate sections as working cords. Tie ten square knots 8" (20.3cm) below the spiral knot sinnet. Repeat to create three more new sections.

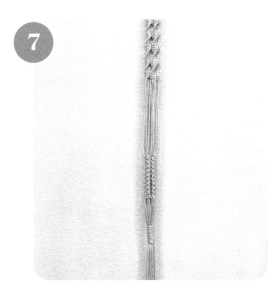

7 Cut one cord to 40" (101.6cm) long. Gather your cords together at the bottom and use the 40" (101.6cm) cord to tie a gathering knot of at least twelve wraps 3" (7.6cm) below the square knot sinnets. Trim the cord ends to 8" (20.3cm). Your plant hanger is now complete!

This design's open spaces allow your plants plenty of room to grow and thrive.

Alternating your working and filler cords from one sinnet to the next over a long space not only creates room for your plant's leaves, but also showcases the natural texture of the fibers.

Ariah Plant Hanger

Do you have a pesky little pet that would love to play with the fringes on your macramé plant hangers? The Ariah plant hanger is the ideal solution! This plant hanger is named after my daughter, who helped me create this "no more pet paws batting at the fringe" design. It's a unique solution for creating a tidy, no-fringe finish.

Materials
- Approximately 100' (30.5m) of 4mm 4-ply twisted cotton macramé cord in your chosen color *(I used Nook Theory color caramel)*
- Two 50mm wooden rings

Knots/Patterns Used
- Reverse lark's head knot
- Square knot
- Half knot (spiral knot sinnet)
- Gathering knot

Instructions

Cut eight cords to 146" (370.8cm). Fold them evenly in half and use reverse lark's head knots to attach them to one of the wooden rings.

Divide the cords into four sections of four cords each. Use the first group of four cords to tie twenty-two square knots.

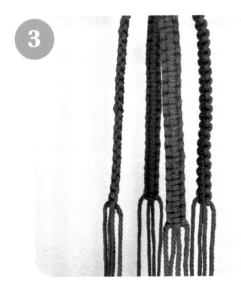

Continue tying twenty-two square knots in the remaining three sections to create a total of four square knot sinnets.

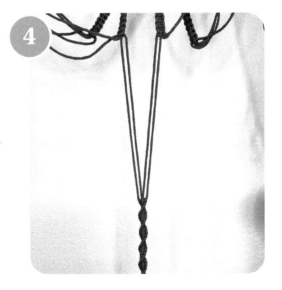

Create a new section by grabbing one inner cord and one outer cord from each of two sections next to each other. Using the two longer cords on the outside, create forty half knots 12" (30.5cm) below the square knot sinnets to create a spiral knot sinnet.

5

Repeat step 4 to create three additional new sections of forty half knots.

6

Flip the plant hanger over and thread the remaining cord through the second wooden ring, leaving around 2" (5.1cm) of cord between the ring and your half knots.

7

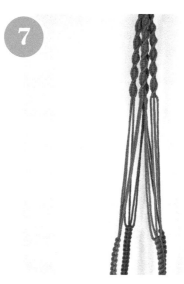

Cut one cord to 30" (76.2cm) and use it to tie a gathering knot of at least eight wraps between the wooden ring and the half knot sinnets. Cut the leftover cord and use your scissors to tuck it into the gathering knot.

This plant hanger is sturdy
and made to support pots in a
range of sizes and shapes.

This gorgeous design blends intricate patterns with perfect functionality.

Coralynn Wall Plant Hanger

Not all plant hangers need to hang from the ceiling—just one reason why I love the Coralynn. This beautiful plant hanger can be displayed right against your wall, providing beautiful support that you and your plant will love! Have fun playing around with the colors on this one—adding a second color to this piece can really make it pop!

Materials

- Approximately 176½' (53.8m) of 4mm single-strand cotton macramé cord in your chosen color (*I used Ganxxet color dusty lavender*)
- 12" x 1" (30.5 x 2.5cm) dowel

Knots/Patterns Used

- Lark's head knot
- Square knot
- Double half hitch knot
- Gathering knot

Instructions

Cut sixteen cords to 128" (325.1cm). Fold them evenly in half and use lark's head knots to attach them to the dowel.

Tie eight rows of decreasing alternating square knots, starting with eight square knots in row one and decreasing in each row to end with one square knot in the center of row 8.

Using the first cord on the left as your filler cord and next cord in as your working cord, tie fifteen diagonal double half hitch knots to the right just below the square knots. Using the last cord on the right side as your filler cord and the next cord in as your working cord, tie sixteen diagonal double half hitch knots to the left to close your point.

Using the first four cords on the left, tie a square knot just below the diagonal double half hitch knots. Repeat with the next twelve cords to create a total of four square knots on the left side. Repeat to create a total of four more square knots on the right side. Using two cords from the bottom two square knots, tie a decreasing alternating square knot in the center.

Using the first cord on the left (cord 1) as your filler cord and the next cord in as your working cord, tie fifteen diagonal double half hitch knots to the right. Gradually leave more space between the square knots and these knots—your first knot will be right against the square knot and your last knot will be about 1" (2.5cm) below the square knots. Using the far cord on the right as your filler cord and the next cord in as your working cord, tie sixteen diagonal double half hitch knots to the left to close your point.

Repeat steps 4 and 5.

Bring the first cord on the left and the last cord on the right to the front to be the filler cords. Bring the second cord in on the left and the second cord in on the right to the front to be the working cords. Tie a square knot approximately 10" (25.4cm) below the bottom point.

Bring the next two cords on the left forward, using the first as your filler cord and the second as your working cord. Using those two cords and the first two cords on the left of the center square knot, tie another square knot just below and to the left. The filler cord from the first square knot will become the right working cord. Repeat on the right side, then repeat once more on each side. You will have a total of six square knots.

This piece is proof that a
decorative wall hanging
can also be useful.

9

Using the four cords in the center, tie an alternating square knot in between the two squares knots on the end to complete the third row. Tie two more rows of decreasing alternating square knots to complete a square knot diamond.

10

Cut a cord to 40" (101.5cm). Gather all the cords at the bottom and use the 40" (101.5cm) cord to tie a gathering knot of at least ten wraps 3" (7.6cm) below your last square knot. Trim the bottom of the cords to 7" (17.8cm).

11

Cut a cord to 30" (76.2cm) and tie a constrictor knot to hang your piece.

Fruit Hangers

Macramé storage solutions are perfect for freeing up counter space in your kitchen in a decorative way.

This hammock is one of the best uses for your new macramé skills—it's decorative and perfectly functional.

Fruit Hammock

Hang your fruit in style with this bohemian macramé fruit hammock. This piece allows you to clear your counters and display your fruit for convenient access. I used four 1" (2.5cm) screw-in cup hooks to hang my fruit hammock under my cabinets.

Materials

- Approximately 70' (21.3m) of 3mm 4-ply twisted cotton macramé cord in your chosen color *(I used Nook Theory color cream)*
- Two 12" x ⅜" (30.5 x 1cm) dowels

Knots/Patterns Used

- Larks head knot
- Square knot
- Overhand knot around dowel
- Half hitch knot

Instructions

Cut ten cords to 84" (213.4cm). Use lark's head knots to attach the cords to one of the dowels in five sections of two knots each. Leave 1" (2.5cm) between each section.

Using the first four cords on the left, tie a square knot. Repeat with the remaining cords until you have a total of five square knots across row one.

Take two cords from the top two square knots and tie an alternating square knot about 1" (2.5cm) below your first row. Repeat three more times until you have a total of four square knots across row 2.

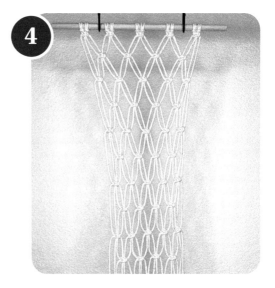

Repeat steps 2 and 3 until you've created a total of eleven rows. Your last row should be five square knots.

5

Wrap cord up around the back of the dowel and out toward the front left

Wrap the cord up around the front of itself and down through the loop, then pull it tight

With your working cords in front of the second dowel, tie an overhand knot around the dowel. Repeat this for each set of cords until you've created a total of ten overhand knots around your dowel.

6

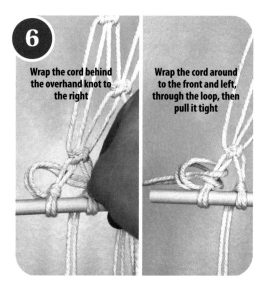

Wrap the cord behind the overhand knot to the right

Wrap the cord around to the front and left, through the loop, then pull it tight

Using the same cords, tie ten half hitch knots above the dowel, on each cord, to secure them.

7

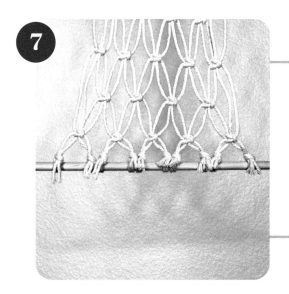

TIP

Attach the outer cords to your dowel first. This will help your hammock hang evenly

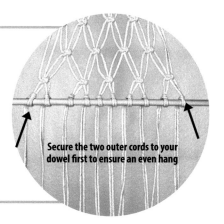

Secure the two outer cords to your dowel first to ensure an even hang

Trim all of the cords, leaving ½" (1.3cm) hanging from the dowel, and enjoy your fruit hammock.

Hanging Fruit Basket

This hanging macramé fruit basket is so practical and looks great hanging in the kitchen. You can make a single basket, but it's also easy to add a second basket if you know you will want more storage. The knotted net is an elegant solution to keep your fruit perfectly ripe.

This design is so versatile—the single basket option works well under lower cabinets, but you can also hang both lengths side by side under standard-height cabinets to add visual interest to your kitchen storage.

Materials

- Approximately 180' (54.9m) for single basket or 359' (109.4m) for double basket of 3mm 4-ply twisted cotton macramé cord in your chosen color (*I used Nook Theory color cream*)

- Two 8" (20.3cm) bamboo hoops per basket
- One 2" (5.1cm) 5mm metal ring

Knots/Patterns Used

- Gathering knot
- Square knot
- Reverse lark's head knot

- Switch knot
- Double half hitch knot around a hoop

Instructions

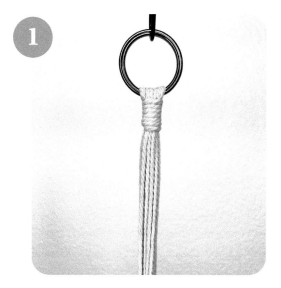

Cut six cords to 84" (213.4cm) and fold them evenly in half through the metal ring. Cut one cord to 18" (30.5cm) and use it to tie a gathering knot of at least six wraps just below the metal ring.

Separate the cords into three sections of four cords each. Tie five square knot sinnets in each section.

Use double half hitch knots to attach the cords around one of the bamboo hoops 4½" (11.4cm) below the square knot sinnets. Leave around 6½" (16.5cm) of space between each section.

Cut thirty cords to 54" (137.2cm) and fold them evenly in half. Use reverse lark's head knots to attach them to the bamboo hoop. Each section should have ten knots.

5

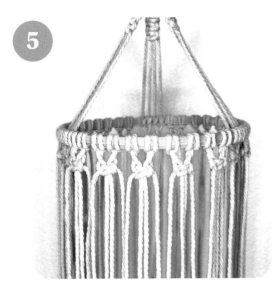

Use the first four cords you attached to the hoop to tie a switch knot ½" (1.3cm) below the bamboo hoop. Repeat this all the way around until you've created a total of eighteen knots (five knots in each of the three sections, and one knot each made with the original hanging cords).

6

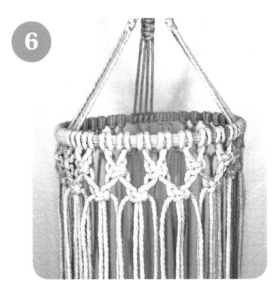

Using a center cord and an outer cord from each of the first two knots, tie an alternating switch knot ½" (1.3cm) below the first row. Repeat this all the way around until you've created a total of eighteen knots.

7

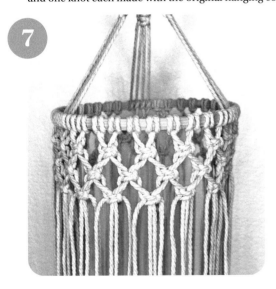

Repeat step 6 to create row 3.

8

Use every hanging cord to tie double half hitch knots around the bamboo hoop just below the third row to attach them. You will create a total of seventy-two knots.

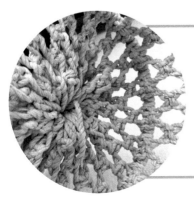

TIP

When tying your gathering knot, you will want to slide the top of the gathering knot cord up through the knots and inside the basket. This will ensure that the knot is made as close to the base as possible. Trim the leftover gathering knot cord inside the basket once your knot is tied.

Repeat steps 5 through 7, but don't leave as much space between the three rows of alternating switch knots. Tie one more row of alternating switch knots so you have a total of four rows.

Cut one cord to 30" (76.2cm) and gather all the hanging cord at the bottom together to create a tight even fit. Use the 30" (76.2cm) cord to tie a tight gathering knot of six to eight wraps around these cords. Trim the bottom cord to 2" (5.1cm). If you are making a single basket, you're done! If you want to create a double basket, continue to the next step.

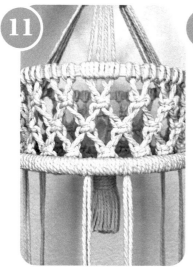

Cut six cords to 84" (213.4cm) and use reverse lark's head knots to attach them to the bottom bamboo hoop. Your cords should be on either side of a switch knot and aligned with the original hanging cords.

Use one of the cord sections to tie a switch knot ½" (1.3 cm) below the bamboo ring. Repeat with the other two sections.

Use double half hitch knots to attach the cords to a third bamboo hoop about 4½" (11.4cm) below the switch knot. Leave around 6½" (16.5cm) of space between each section. Repeat steps 4 through 10 to create the second fruit basket.

A mix of single and double hanging fruit baskets adds a ton of fruit-and-vegetable-friendly storage!

This is a simple design that will keep your bananas perfectly delicious for much longer.

Beaded Banana Hanger

Did you know that your bananas will last longer if you hang them? Hanging them slows down the ripening process, allowing you to keep your bananas longer. This banana hanger is convenient, effective, and looks great in the kitchen.

Materials

- Approximately 80" (203.2cm) of 3mm 4-ply twisted cotton macramé cord in your chosen color (*I used Nook Theory color olive*)
- Six 14mm wooden beads with 3.5mm interior hole

Knots/Patterns Used

- Overhand knot
- Square knot

Sometimes a quick, simple
design is exactly what you
need to do the job.

Instructions

1 Cut two cords to 20" (50.8cm). Fold one evenly in half and hang it on a hook. Fold the second cord evenly in half and use it to tie an overhand knot 1" (2.5cm) down on the first cord.

2 Cut one cord to 30" (76.2cm), fold it evenly in half, and tie five square knots with multiple filler cords around all the cords just below the overhand knot.

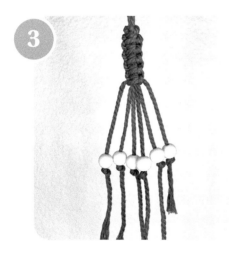

3 Slide a bead onto one of the cords about 3" (7.6cm) below the last square knot and secure it in place with an overhand knot. Repeat with the remaining five cords.

4 Trim the cords to 1" (2.5cm) and enjoy!

TIP

Use a beading tool (I use the EZ Beader shown here) to help slide your beads onto your cord. If you do not have one, a tapestry needle or even a bobby pin will work.

Macramé shelves can help you stay organized while transforming your jewelry into a part of the decor.

Shelves

Arvin Wall Shelf

This wall shelf is such a statement piece for your home, combining art with function. Display some of your favorite decorative items and enjoy the look of this beauty every time you see it! Be careful to level your shelf before tightening your knots below the drilled holes—you want to make sure your shelf is beautiful and functional!

Macramé wall shelves are gorgeous solutions if you need more vertical display space for plants, tchotchkes, or pretty much anything else.

Materials

- Approximately 362½' (110.5m) of 4mm 4-ply twisted cotton macramé cord in your chosen color (*I used AIFUN color natural*)
- 26" x 1" (66 x 2.5cm) piece of driftwood or dowel
- 26" x 6" x 1" (66 x 15.3 x 2.5cm) wood board
- Drill with ⁵⁄₁₆" drill bit

Knots/Patterns Used

- Lark's head knot
- Square knot
- Double half hitch knot
- Reverse lark's head knot
- Half knot sinnet (spiral knot)

Instructions

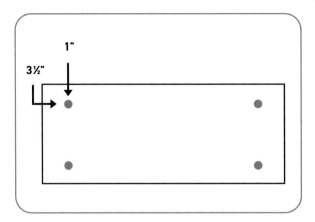

Shelf measurements—be sure to measure on all four sides prior to drilling.

1

Cut eighteen cords to 86" (218.5cm). Fold them evenly in half and use lark's head knots to attach them to the center of the driftwood or dowel.

2 Group 1 Group 2 Group 3

Working in groups of twelve cords, tie three groups of decreasing alternating square knots. You will create three rows in each group, starting with three knots and finishing with one knot.

3

In groups 1 and 2, use the farthest cord on the right as your filler cord and tie five diagonal double half hitch knots to the left just below the square knots. Use the first cord on the left as your filler cord and tie six diagonal double half hitch knots to the right to close the point. In group 3, use first cord on the left as your filler cord and tie five diagonal double half hitch knots to the right. Use the farthest cord on the right as your filler cord and tie six diagonal double half hitch knots to the left to close the point.

Using cords 11, 12, 13, and 14 and cords 23, 24, 25, and 26, tie two four-cluster square knot diamonds.

Using cord 18 as your filler cord, tie five diagonal double half hitch knots to the left. Use cord 7 as your filler cord and tie six diagonal double half hitch knots to the right to close the point. Use cord 19 as your filler cord and tie five diagonal double half hitch knots to the right. Use cord 30 as your filler cord and tie six diagonal double half hitch knots to close the point.

Using cords 17, 18, 19, and 20, tie another four-cluster square knot diamond. Using cord 13 as your filler cord, tie five diagonal double half hitch knots to the right. Using cord 24 as your filler cord, tie six diagonal double half hitch knots to the left to close the point.

Cut four cords to 140" (355.6cm) and use lark's head knots to attach them evenly to the left side of your work. Tie a square knot using cords 3 and 6 as your working cords. Using cord 8 as your filler cord, tie three diagonal double half hitch knots to the left. Using cord 1 as your filler cord, tie seven diagonal double half hitch knots to the right. Using cord 8 as the filler cord, tie three more diagonal double half hitch knots to the left. (See Double Half Hitch Diamond with Accent Knot on page 39.)

8 Repeat the double half hitch diamond with accent knot pattern from step 7 until you've created four full diamonds. End with a half diamond and square knot. Repeat step 7 on the right side and fill in the remaining pattern.

9 Using cord 8 from the left piece as your filler cord and cord 1 from the right piece as your working cord, tie one diagonal double half hitch knot to join the two half diamonds.

10 Release the working cord and use the same filler cord to tie three more diagonal double half hitch knots to the right with the next three cords to the right just below the square knot. Pick up the original working cord you'd set aside and use it as the filler cord to tie three diagonal double half hitch knots to the left just below the square knot. Tie a square knot in the center using the four center cords.

11 Using the farthest cord on the left as the filler cord, tie seven diagonal double half hitch knots to the right. Using the farthest cord on the right as the filler cord on the left and tie 8 diagonal double half hitch knots to the left to close the heart. Trim the cords below the point to 13" (33cm).

Cut thirty cords to 32" (81.3cm). Fold them evenly in half and use reverse lark's head knots to attach them to the bottom loops of the diamond accents. Attach three cords in each loop. You will have fifteen cords on each side.

Cut four cords to 130" (330.2cm). Use lark's head knots to attach two cords to the left side of the driftwood or dowel. Keep the filler cords hanging to 27" (68.6cm). Repeat on the right side. On the left side, tie eighty left-facing half knots to create a right-twisting spiral knot. On the right side, tie eighty right-facing half knots to create a left-twisting spiral knot. Use the working cords from the right side to tie three right-facing half knots around all the cords to join both sides. Trim the bottom of the cords to align with the other cords.

Cut four cords to 145" (368.3cm). Use lark's head knots to attach two cords to the left side of the driftwood or dowel. Keep the filler cords hanging to 25" (63.5cm). Tie eighty-five left-facing half knots to create a right-twisting spiral knot that is about 17½" (44.5cm) long. Repeat on the right side, using right-facing half knots to create a left-twisting spiral knot.

Repeat step 14, but tie only eighty-two half knots on each side to create spiral knots that are each 17" (43.2cm) long.

16

If you haven't already, measure and drill the holes in the wood board as shown on page 117. Thread all four cords of each spiral knot through the corresponding shelf holes so that the last knot is right against the wood. Match the inner spiral knots to the front holes and the outer spiral knots with the back holes. Tie five half knots directly below the wood board to secure it (use a level to make sure your shelf Is even before you pull the knots tight). Untwist the cords.

17

Cut a cord to your preferred length and tie a constrictor knot on each side of the wood to create a hanging cord.

This wall hanging blends a variety of knots and patterns to create a bohemian backdrop for your favorite plants and display pieces.

Stella Jewelry Shelf

This bohemian handmade shelf is perfect for displaying your favorite jewelry. It's an eye-catching piece that you will always smile about while grabbing your necklaces or bracelets. Displaying some of your favorite crystals or plants is a nice choice, too! This is a straightforward no-drill shelf design.

This simple design combines diamonds with accent beads to amplify the natural beauty of cords and wood.

Materials

- Approximately 97' (29.6m) of 3mm 3-ply twisted cotton macramé cord in your chosen color *(I used Ganxxet color natural)*
- 19½" x 1¼" (49.5 x 3cm) piece of driftwood
- Ten 20mm wooden beads with 10mm interior hole
- Three 1" (2.5cm) screw hooks
- 19" x 3½" x 1" (48.3 x 8.9 x 2.5cm) wood board

Knots/Patterns Used

- Lark's head knot
- Double half hitch knot
- Gathering knot

Instructions

Cut four cords to 128" (325.1cm) and use lark's head knots to attach them 3" (7.6cm) in on the left side of your driftwood.

Using cord 1 as your filler cord, tie three diagonal double half hitch knots to the right.

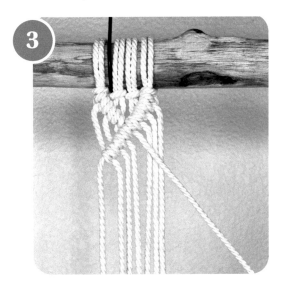

Using cord 8 as your filler cord, tie seven diagonal double half hitch knots to the left.

Using cord 5 as your filler cord, tie three diagonal double half hitch knots to the right.

5

Add one of the wooden beads to the two center cords (cords 4 and 5).

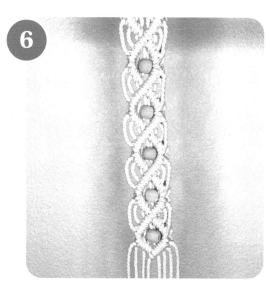

6

Repeat steps 2 through 5 to create a total of five diamonds. On your last diamond, tie only four diagonal double half hitch knots to the left (rather than seven) to close the diamond.

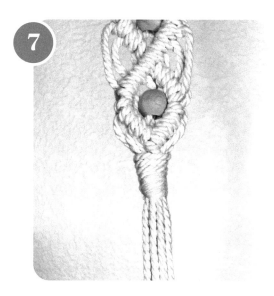

7

Cut one cord to 24" (61cm) and tie a gathering knot of at least eight wraps around all the cords just below the last diamond.

8

Repeat steps 1 through 7 on the right side of the driftwood.

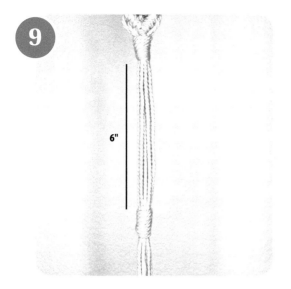

Cut two cords to 24" (61cm). Use one of the cords to tie a gathering knot of at least eight wraps 6" (15.2cm) below the first gathering knot. Repeat on the other side.

Trim the cord to 6" (15.2cm). Unravel the cords.

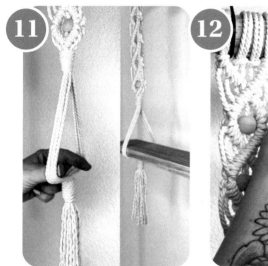

Separate the cords between the two gathering knots so that you have four cords in the front and four cords in the back. Slide the wood board into these openings on each side.

Twist the screw hooks into the driftwood, spacing them evenly between the two macramé sections. I used three in my finished shelf, but you can add as many as you'd like.

Cut one cord to 42" (106.7cm) and tie a constrictor knot in the middle of the cords on each side of the driftwood to create a hanging cord. Sit back and enjoy your shelf!

I use my shelf to display my favorite crystals and beautiful colorful jewelry pieces that double as wall art.

Index

#

3-ply twisted cord, 23
4-ply twisted cord, 23

A

abbreviations (knots), 27
alternating square knot, 38
angel, 19

B

beads, 22, 25, 39
   adding, 45
bookmark, 9
brush, 25

C

cat bed, 78
clothing rack, 24
clove hitch knot, 31
coasters, 15
comb, 25
constrictor knot, 35
continuous lark's head knots
   around a ring, 42
cord, 22, 23
   how much is needed, 45
   leftover, 46
cotton macramé cord, 23

D

diagonal double half hitch
   knot, 31, 39, 40, 41
double half hitch around a
   ring or dowel, 41
double half hitch diamond
   with accent knot, 39
double half hitch knot, 31
double half hitch leaf, 40

dowel, 25
   double half hitch around,
   41
driftwood, 25
   cleaning (tip), 25
dyeing macramé, 72

E

earrings, 18

F

feather, 16, 18, 61
   earrings, 18
   wall hanging, 16
filler cord(s), 26
four-cluster square knot
   diamond, 37
four-ply twisted cord, 23

G

garland, 13
gathering knot, 33

H

half knot sinnet, 37
half knot, 29
hat holder, 20
hoops, 24

K

knots, common
   abbreviations, 27

L

lark's head knot, 28
left-facing half knot, 29
left-facing square knot, 30

M

macramé cord, 22, 23
   how much is needed, 45
   leftover, 46
macramé, cleaning, 44
measuring tape, 22, 24
mini plant hanger, 11
mirror frame, 21

O

ornament, 19
overhand knot, 34

P

plant hanger, 11, 14, 20, 86,
  90, 94, 98
   for wall, 98
   mini, 11
pumpkin, 17

R

reef knot, 32
reverse lark's head knot, 28
right-facing half knot, 29
right-facing square knot, 30
rings, wooden, 22, 24
   double half
   hitch around, 41

S

S hooks, 22
scissors, 22, 24
shelf, 116, 122
single-strand cord, 23
sinnet, 26
spiral knot, 37
square knot sinnet, 36

square knot, 29
   with multiple filler
   cords, 36
   with multiple
   working cords, 36
switch knot, 30

T

tape measure, 22, 24
tassels, making, 34
three-ply twisted cord, 23
tips and tricks, 44
twisted cord, 23
   unraveling, 26, 45

U

unravel, 26, 45

W

wall hanging, 9, 10, 12, 13,
  16, 18, 20, 48, 54, 61, 66
   dyed, 72
wooden rings, 22
working cord(s), 26
wrap knot, 33

Z

zigzag, 41

About the Author

Angela Barretta, a self-taught macramé artist, discovered her passion for the craft through her love and addiction to houseplants. Once she delved into macramé, she never looked back, finding inspiration in teaching and launching a business to sell her creations. Designing new patterns and projects kept her creative mind engaged. When not immersed in her business, Angela enjoys spending time with her husband, two kids, and their dogs, and tending to her flourishing collection of houseplants. You can connect with Angela on Instagram, TikTok, Facebook, YouTube, Pinterest, and Etsy @AngsCraftsnCreations.

Acknowledgments

Thank you to my husband and kids who have shown tremendous support throughout this journey. Thank you to my wonderful daughter Ariah, my niece Abigail, and my sister-in law Alex who helped with some of my photos—I had so much fun with you! And a big thank-you to all the creators out there! I hope you love this book as much as I do.